Road to
Reading

Road to Reading

A Program for Preventing & Remediating Reading Difficulties

by

Benita A. Blachman, Ph.D.
Syracuse University, New York

and

Darlene M. Tangel, Ph.D.
Syracuse University, New York
Oriskany Central School District, New York

Baltimore • London • Sydney

Paul H. Brookes Publishing Co.
Post Office Box 10624
Baltimore, Maryland 21285-0624

www.brookespublishing.com

Typeset by Maryland Composition Company, Laurel, Maryland.
Manufactured in China by JADE PRODUCTIONS.

Original illustrations by Jane Freeman.
Third printing, December 2015.

Library of Congress Cataloging-in-Publication Data

Blachman, Benita A.
  Road to reading : a program for preventing and remediating reading difficulties / by Benita A. Blachman, and Darlene M. Tangel.
     p.   cm.
  Includes bibliographical references.
  ISBN-13: 978-1-55766-904-9 (spiral bound)
  ISBN-10: 1-55766-904-X (spiral bound)
  1. Reading—Remedial teaching. I. Tangel, Darlene M. II. Title.
  LB1050.5.B514 2008
  372.46—dc22   2007035550

British Library Cataloguing in Publication data are available from the British Library.

Contents

CD-ROM Contents

About This CD-ROM

Contents

Lesson Plan Forms

    Daily Lesson Plan

    Weekly Lesson Plan

    Daily Evaluation and Attendance Form

Assessment Forms

    Letter Name and Sound Assessment

    Levels Assessment

        Levels Assessment Directions

        Levels Assessment Recording Form

        Levels Assessment Student Reading Pages

        • *Red Level*

        • *Orange Level*

        • *Yellow Level*

        • *Green Level—Group I Vowel Teams*

        • *Green Level—Group II Vowel Teams*

        • *Blue Level*

        • *Purple Level*

    High Frequency Word Assessments

        Red Level

        Orange Level

        Yellow Level

        Green Level

        Blue Level

        Purple Level

Step 1 Materials

    Sound Pack Cards: Consonants

    Sound Pack Cards: Vowels

    Blank Sound Pack Cards

Step 2 Materials

    Directions for Making a Sound Board and Letter Cards

    Sound Board Consonants

    Sound Board Vowels

        Vowels

        Vowel Teams

        Vowel + r

    Sound Board Digraphs

    Blank Letter Cards

About the Authors

Benita A. Blachman, Ph.D., Trustee Professor of Education and Psychology, School of Education and College of Arts and Sciences, Syracuse University, Syracuse, New York

Benita A. Blachman is Trustee Professor of Education and Psychology at Syracuse University, with appointments in Reading and Language Arts, Special Education, and Psychology. She also holds a courtesy appointment in the Communication Sciences and Disorders Department. She has a doctoral degree in educational psychology from the University of Connecticut and is a former special education teacher, reading specialist, and learning disabilities consultant. She has published extensively in the area of early literacy, focusing her research on early intervention to prevent reading failure and on the factors that predict reading achievement. Dr. Blachman's research has been funded by the National Institute of Child Health and Human Development, the U.S. Department of Education Institute of Education Sciences, and the National Center for Learning Disabilities. Dr. Blachman serves on the professional advisory boards of the National Dyslexia Research Foundation and the Neuhaus Center.

Darlene M. Tangel, Ph.D., Reading Specialist and Chairperson, Committee on Special Education, Oriskany Central District, Oriskany, New York, and Adjunct Assistant Professor, School of Education, Syracuse University, Syracuse, New York

Darlene M. Tangel is an adjunct assistant professor in the Reading and Language Arts Department at Syracuse University. She has taught graduate courses in learning disabilities and in language disorders at Syracuse University and has been a reading specialist in the Oriskany Public Schools for more than 25 years, where she also serves as the Chair of Special Education and Chair of Preschool Special Education. Her research interests include early reading acquisition and invented spelling, alternative reading curricula for children at risk for reading failure, and adult literacy. She has developed training materials for the American Federation of Teachers and has extensive experience conducting teacher training workshops. The focus of these workshops is translating research into practical application for classroom use. Dr. Tangel has been cited numerous times in Who's Who Among America's Teachers.

Drs. Tangel and Blachman were awarded the Dina Feitelson Research Award by the International Reading Association for their research on invented spelling. They are also coauthors with Eileen Wynne Ball and Rochella Black of *Road to the Code: A Phonological Awareness Program for Young Children,* published by Paul H. Brookes Publishing Co.

Preface and Acknowledgments

Road to Reading: A Program for Preventing and Remediating Reading Difficulties is the result of research conducted since the 1980s. In an early study, one of us (Blachman, 1987), worked with primary grade teachers to create a program that could be used in general education classrooms with children who were having difficulty learning to read. In later studies (e.g., Blachman, Tangel, Ball, Black, & McGraw, 1999; Tangel & Blachman, 1995), we found that students in first grade who participated in this program (as well as phonological awareness activities and letter sound instruction in kindergarten) in general education classrooms for 30 minutes each day were better readers at the end of first and second grade than similar children who did not participate in this program.

We were pleased when the National Reading Panel (National Institute of Child Health and Human Development, 2000) included the results from our studies (specifically, Ball & Blachman, 1991; Blachman, Ball, Black, & Tangel, 1994; Blachman et al., 1999; and Tangel & Blachman, 1992) in their report and concluded that our studies (among many others) added to the converging evidence supporting the value of phoneme awareness and phonics instruction when teaching children to read.

In a more recent study (Blachman et al., 2004), we expanded the 30- to 40-minute lessons found in this book to 50-minute lessons used with struggling readers in second and third grade. After 8 months, children who participated in the program made significantly greater gains in reading and spelling than the children who did not participate in this program.

As you will learn when you read the Introduction, the program has been used by teachers in a variety of settings. It is flexible and will enable the teacher to provide scientifically based reading instruction to all children.

Many wonderful colleagues have contributed to our work over the years. We would especially like to thank Dr. Eileen Ball and Rochella Black for their contributions as coauthors on some of our earlier articles and as coauthors on our phonological awareness program, *Road to the Code: A Phonological Awareness Program for Young*

Children, published in 2000 by Paul H. Brookes Publishing Co. Dr. Sheila Clonan provided feedback on a previous version of this program and was a coauthor on our 2004 study. We would like to express our heartfelt thanks to her as well.

In addition, many extraordinary teachers who have participated in our research studies over the years have provided valuable feedback that contributed to the creation of *Road to Reading*. We would like to thank Kelli Johnson for her suggestions regarding the types of prepared materials that would make this program more teacher friendly. Many of those materials were included on a CD-ROM prepared for a prepublication version by Joseph Portelli. Vicki McQuitty edited many of the lists of additional materials used in this program.

The completion of this project was due, in part, to the dedicated effort and expertise of two special people. Maria Murray provided editorial feedback every step of the way and coordinated the production of all aspects of a prepublication version of this program. Angelique Van Boden was responsible for the design and format of the prepublication version.

Finally, we wish to express our appreciation to Jessica Allan, Sarah Shepke, Janet Wehner, and the entire staff at Paul H. Brookes Publishing Co. for their support for this project and encouragement and assistance throughout the publication process.

Benita A. Blachman and Darlene M. Tangel
Syracuse, New York

Introduction

Two consensus panels (Snow et al., 1998; National Institute of Child Health and Human Development [NICHD], 2000) provided a much needed blueprint for early reading practices proven to reduce the number of students who experience difficulty learning to read. The practices include, among others, instruction in phonological awareness, the alphabetic principle, and accurate and fluent word recognition, as well as frequent opportunities for text-based reading with corrective feedback to build motivation and comprehension strategies.

Road to Reading embraces these practices and provides a framework for providing both early intervention to prevent reading difficulties and remedial instruction for students who are struggling to learn to read.

Goals of the Program

An important objective of this program is to help develop accurate and fluent word identification. The emphasis is on explicit, systematic, **research-based** instruction to help students understand the alphabetic principle (i.e., how individual letters and letter combinations represent spoken language sounds). The word recognition skills introduced provide the essential foundation and support for good reading comprehension.

Accurate and fluent word identification can be developed, in part, by learning the six basic syllable patterns. This program provides an overview of the structure of the English language by introducing the six syllable patterns and the most common phonetic elements. The six syllable patterns include the following:

- Closed syllables (as in h*at* and fl*ag*)

- Final "e" syllables (as in l*ake* and sl*ide*)

- Open syllables (as in **he** and the first syllable of **si**l*ent*)

- Vowel team syllables (as in tr*ain*, l*eaf*, and cl*own*)

- Vowel + r syllables (as in c*ar*, h*orn*, and p*er*ch)

- Consonant + le (as in sim**ple** and tum**ble**)

All of the syllable patterns will be learned as the students progress through the six levels of the program. These patterns will be practiced by the students when they read decodable texts and also reinforced as they read a wide variety of trade books and books representing various genres.

The goal in teaching these patterns is for students to begin to read appropriate grade level texts fluently and with good comprehension as early as possible.

Is This a Complete Reading Program?

Although this is not a complete *classroom* reading program, it can be used in conjunction with any reading series. For example, although the program includes specific high frequency words (Fry & Kress, 2006), one could substitute high frequency words from any basal series or list. In addition, decodable books from any series can be substituted for the decodable books on our book charts. Likewise, basal anthologies and leveled books could be substituted for the trade books on our trade book list.

We have woven vocabulary throughout this program by highlighting words and encouraging teachers to use daily opportunities to extend vocabulary. We do not, however, include specific instructions for teaching vocabulary. Because teachers will be selecting books from various sources, choices about which vocabulary words to teach should be based on the needs of the students and the books the students are reading.

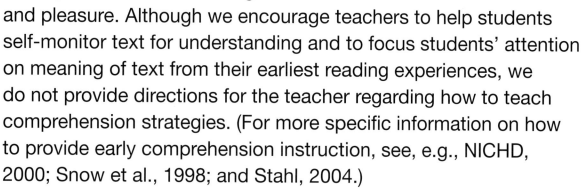

The program includes frequent opportunities to read and reread both narrative and expository text with corrective feedback to develop fluency, build comprehension strategies, and foster reading for information and pleasure. Although we encourage teachers to help students self-monitor text for understanding and to focus students' attention on meaning of text from their earliest reading experiences, we do not provide directions for the teacher regarding how to teach comprehension strategies. (For more specific information on how to provide early comprehension instruction, see, e.g., NICHD, 2000; Snow et al., 1998; and Stahl, 2004.)

Who Is This Program For?

This five-step research-based program has been used with groups of varying sizes in a variety of settings, such as general education classrooms, remedial reading programs, resource rooms, and one-to-one tutoring. If you are using this program during the English language arts block, the lessons should take about 30–40 minutes. We recommend that the group size not exceed six students.

This program has also been used with small groups of three to six students and with individual students (one-to-one) who are not meeting grade level benchmarks in their classroom reading program or on statewide assessments. These students have been taught by general education teachers, reading teachers, and special education teachers both in and out of the general classroom setting. In a recently reported tutoring study using this program (Blachman et al., 2004), lessons were expanded to 50 minutes to provide more sustained and intensive instruction for second- and third-grade struggling readers. This program can also be adapted for use with older students by adding more multisyllabic words at each level and by including age-appropriate trade books.

This program has proven to be flexible in a variety of settings and will allow the teacher to provide *scientifically-based* reading instruction to all students.

Pacing

A critical factor in the success of a young child learning to read is proper pacing of instruction. There are many pacing decisions (e.g., how many times a word needs to be reviewed, how many times a book needs to be reread to develop fluency) that only you will be able to make as you get to know your students.

Teachers have often asked how long it takes to complete this program. There is not one right answer to this question. The speed with which students complete the program will depend on their initial skill level, their rate of learning, and whether this program is being used for early intervention with students in first grade in a general education classroom or as a remedial program with somewhat older students (Grades 2–4) who have already experienced difficulty learning to read.

As you use this program, you will become more skilled at knowing when your students are ready to move on and when they need more practice. If you have questions about your students' readiness to move on, adjust your lesson plan for the next day and include some of the more challenging material as a diagnostic tool to help you make your decision.

Progress Monitoring

Regular progress monitoring is a critically important component of instruction. The notes that you make on your daily lesson plans, as well as the more formal assessments used by your district, will help you evaluate the success of each student in your group on an ongoing basis. To help you get started with progress monitoring, we have created a brief assessment for each level. These assessments can be found on the accompanying CD-ROM ◑.

Getting Ready to Use the Program

The Six Levels

The best way to get started is to **familiarize yourself with the six levels** of the program. Each level includes the following:

• A list of goals for that level

• Text that will guide your teaching

• Additional materials to help you plan your daily lessons

You will see that each of the six levels is color coded using the colors of the rainbow: red, orange, yellow, green, blue, purple (we cheated a bit and collapsed indigo and violet—the last two colors in the "proper" rainbow—into purple).

Each level, starting with Red, increases in difficulty and builds on the previous level. In the Red Level, students begin the program by reviewing consonants, learning short vowels, and learning the first set of high frequency words.

The Five-Step Plan

The daily lesson for each level includes five steps. As students move through each level of the program, the Five-Step Plan remains the same. *That is, the content of each daily lesson increases in difficulty, but the five steps used to teach the content will always be the same.*

1. **Review sound–symbol correspondences**
   Review sound–symbol associations and introduce new sounds.

2. **Teach or review new decoding skill**
   Practice making words to develop a new decoding skill (e.g., building words with the final "e" pattern), reinforcing both phonemic awareness and phonics skills.

3. **Review phonetically regular words (PRWs) and high frequency words (HFWs)**
   Review previously learned phonetically regular words and high frequency words, with an emphasis on fluency and opportunities to extend vocabulary.

4. **Read orally in context**
   Read orally narrative and expository text for fluency and comprehension.

5. **Dictation**
   Spell words from earlier steps in the lesson.

Lesson Plans and Materials

Before you teach each lesson, you will need to prepare your *lesson plan* and gather the *materials* needed to teach each of the five steps.

Lesson Plan

A blank lesson plan form (see sample provided) can be printed from the CD-ROM . The lesson plan is set up according to the five steps of the lesson. Each step on the plan has spaces for you to write exactly which letter sounds, words, sentences, and books you will be using in each lesson. Appendix A contains three sample lesson plans for each of the six levels. Each level of the program also includes lists and charts to assist you in preparing your lessons.

Materials

The following is an overview of the materials needed for each step of the lesson:

1. Review sound–symbol correspondences

Materials: You will need a sound pack that contains sound cards for review and cards with any new sound(s) to be introduced. Sound cards can be found on the accompanying CD-ROM 🔘 and just need to be printed.

2. Teach or review new decoding skill

Materials: You will need a sound board for each student. Directions for making the sound board are on the accompanying CD-ROM 🔘. The letter cards to use on the sound board are also on the CD-ROM 🔘 and just need to be printed. Sample word lists are provided for each level of the program.

3. Review phonetically regular words (PRWs) and high frequency words (HFWs)

Materials: You will need a word card pack of phonetically regular words and high frequency words. Word cards for the word card pack are on the accompanying CD-ROM 🔘 and just need to be printed. Sample word lists are provided for each level of the program.

4. Reading orally in context

Materials: We have provided lists of decodable books and trade books. You can select from these materials or from whatever series and trade books you have available.

5. Dictation

Materials: Each student needs a dictation notebook (not provided). Sample dictation exercises are provided for each level of the program.

Also included on the accompanying CD-ROM ◐ are numerous forms (e.g., an evaluation and attendance form, assessment forms, blank lesson plans) to help you plan your lessons and monitor progress.

Prerequisite Skills for This Program

As you look through the program, you will see that we start in the Red Level by teaching the students letter names and sounds. Next, we use those sounds to practice phoneme analysis and blending by manipulating letter cards on a sound board to create new words reflecting a particular syllable pattern (e.g., closed syllables like _hid_ and _ship_).

Students who can demonstrate beginning levels of phoneme awareness (e.g., can orally segment two- and three-phoneme words like _up_ and _sun_) and who know some letter names and sounds are ready to begin the Red Level.

Students who cannot yet segment two-phoneme words and who have limited knowledge of letter names and sounds may need some additional phoneme awareness activities before beginning the program, _especially if the students are in kindergarten or just beginning first grade._ There are several published programs that can be used for this purpose. Two such programs are _Road to the Code_ (Blachman, Ball, Black, & Tangel, 2000) and _Phonemic Awareness in Young Children_ (Adams, Foorman, Lundberg, & Beeler, 1998).

For other first grade students and older students with limited phoneme awareness, we suggest you begin the Red Level in the program and incorporate phoneme awareness activities as a "warm up" activity for a few weeks at the beginning of each daily five-step lesson.

We suggest adding a short (3- to 5-minute) phoneme awareness activity called *Say-It-and-Move-It* (Blachman et al., 2000) for these students.

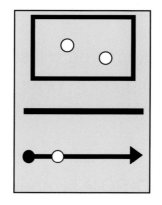

Say-It-and-Move-It activity.
Adapted from *Road to the Code*.

This activity provides an opportunity for students to move discs to represent the sounds in two- and three-phoneme spoken words. A complete description of these activities can be found in the program titled *Road to the Code* (Blachman et al., 2000).

For students who need this additional short-term instruction in phoneme awareness when they start the Red Level, we have selected a subset of the *Say-It-and-Move-It* lessons from the 44 lessons in *Road to the Code*: Lessons 1, 2, 3, 5, 11, 12, 14, 15, 17, 18, 19, 20, 22, 25, 32, 35, 39, and 43.

After each day's phoneme awareness warm-up, your group can do a somewhat shorter version of the Five-Step Plan. During the time you are including *Say-It-and-Move-It,* less time might be spent on Step 3 (review phonetically regular words and high frequency words) and Step 4 (read orally in context). More time could be spent, however, reviewing and teaching the letter sounds in Step 1, using phoneme analysis and blending skills to build words on the sound board in Step 2, and writing dictated words in Step 5.

> ### *Please note:*
>
> - Throughout this program, you will see individual letters set off by slanted lines (e.g., /s/). When you see these slanted lines, they indicate that you should use the letter sound, not the letter name.
>
> - When you see the CD-ROM symbol ◐, it indicates that materials (or directions to make materials) for that step in the lesson are available on the accompanying CD-ROM.
>
> - When you see the puzzle icon 🧩🧩🧩🧩🧩🧩, it indicates one of the many opportunities for integrating this program with other reading materials you may be using in your classroom.

Red Level

Goals for the Red Level

When the students complete this level, they should be able to do the following:

⭐ 1 Identify all consonant sounds.

⭐ 2 Identify the five short vowel sounds (/a/, /i/, /o/, /u/, and /e/).

⭐ 3 Read and spell closed syllable words (e.g., b<u>a</u>t, s<u>i</u>t, h<u>o</u>t, r<u>u</u>n, f<u>e</u>d).

⭐ 4 Identify the digraphs *th, ch, sh,* and *-ck.*

⭐ 5 Read and spell closed syllable words with the digraphs *th, ch, sh,* and *-ck* (e.g., **<u>th</u>ick, <u>sh</u>in, <u>ch</u>ick**).

An Important Note About Teaching High Frequency Words

In each level of the program, students will be introduced to new decoding/phonics skills and also to new high frequency words (e.g., *said*). Although the phonics skills build on one another (e.g., *lip* becomes *slip*), the high frequency words do not. Assigning specific high frequency words to a particular level of the program is arbitrary; it is just meant to be a guide to help you organize your teaching.

Questions

Q: **What if the students in one of my groups don't know all of the high frequency words at one level but are ready to move on to the next level of the program in terms of their decoding skills?**

A: You may find that you have a group in which most of the students learn the decoding/phonics skills at a particular level but do not know all of the high frequency words listed for that level. These students should move on to the next level of the program—the Orange Level—but you should continue to reinforce the high frequency words from the Red Level by continuing to include them in your word card pack. The high frequency words can also be reinforced in whole group instruction using a word wall or be sent home for review.

Q: **What if the students already know all of the high frequency words at one level but are *not* ready to move on to the next level of the program in terms of their decoding skills?**

A: If students already know all of the high frequency words in one level of the program before learning all of the decoding skills at that level, simply begin to introduce the high frequency words from the next level in the program.

Remember!

Students will be expected to learn the decoding skills in one level before going on to the next level; however, it is not necessary for students to learn all of the high frequency words at a particular level before moving to the next level.

Step 1

3 minutes

Review Sound–Symbol Correspondences

Materials

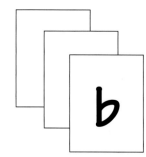

CD Sound pack cards (sounds for review and new sounds)

Procedures

To get started with Step 1, you will need current information about the letter–sound knowledge of your students. If you don't have this information, you should administer the Letter Name and Sound Assessment 💿, which includes the consonants, short vowels (/a/, /i/, /o/, /u/, and /e/), and digraphs (*th, ch, sh,* and *-ck*) that will be taught at this level.

The consonants, short vowels, and digraphs can each be put on separate cards to create a sound pack that can be used both for the assessment and for Step 1.

Select previously learned letters from the sound pack, and quickly review the letter names and sounds.

One way of doing this is to hold the pack of cards so that all of the students in the group can see the top card.

It is a good idea to write a key word for each sound (especially the vowels) on the back of each card so that the same key word is used every time.

> **Please note:** You do not need to review each sound each day. You will have about 10–15 cards in your pack each day. Include some sounds that have been mastered (these can be rotated) and a few that the students are still learning. **Each student in the group should get at least two to three turns.**

- Ask one student for the letter name and sound and a word that starts with that sound.

- For vowels, ask the student for the name, sound, and key word (e.g., *a* says /a/ as in **a**pple, *i* says /i/ as in **i**tch, *o* says /o/ as in **o**ctopus, *u* says /u/ as in **u**p, *e* says /e/ as in **E**d).

- Then, flip that card to the back of the pack, go on to the next card, and ask the next student for the name and sound of the letter on the new card.

- If a student makes an error, provide the correct letter name, sound, and word that starts with that sound, and have the student repeat the correct response.

- Make note of any missed items on your lesson plan. Make sure those items are included in the sound pack the next day.

- Continue until the pack is completed, moving quickly from student to student.

> It is important to move quickly. The objective is to develop fluency while keeping this activity from becoming tedious. You might want to repeat the pack twice if you feel more practice is needed.

- Continue to add new sounds to the sound pack as each sound is introduced.

- As you teach the new sounds, also have the student give words that begin with each letter sound.

- Introduce only one new short vowel at a time. Be sure to use the key words provided for the short vowels. Do not add a new vowel until the current vowel has been learned by most of the students.

- Add the digraphs *th, ch, sh,* and *-ck* to the sound pack one at a time. Each digraph makes a single sound, as in the words **_th_**in, **_ch_**ip, **_sh_**ip, and so**_ck_**.

Step 2

Teach or Review New Decoding Skill

5–7 minutes

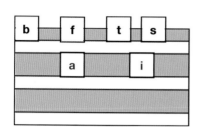

Materials

 Sound board for each student

 Consonant letters in the top pocket (only include those letters needed to make words for a particular lesson)

 Vowel letters in the middle pocket (only include those letters needed to make words for a particular lesson)

Procedures

In Step 2, you will be using a sound board to help students learn to build words with new phonetic patterns and to read the words accurately.

Use the procedure on the next page to introduce the sound board. This procedure will help students learn to blend sounds (e.g., pronouncing the first consonant and vowel, /sa/, of the word *sat* as one unit) to avoid the distortion of sounding out words letter by letter.

- First, slowly pronounce a word such as **sat**, emphasizing the medial vowel.

- Ask the students to repeat the word, listen for the vowel sound, select the vowel letter card (color-coded for a vowel) from the middle pocket, and place the vowel letter card in the lower pocket of the chart.

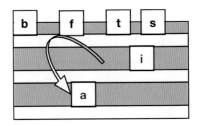

- Repeat the whole word, and ask the students for the initial sound.

- Ask the students to select the appropriate letter card, identify it, and place it in front of the vowel.

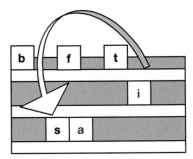

- Draw your finger along the two letters that the students have placed in the lower pocket, and pronounce the sounds as a unit (e.g., "Now, we have /sa/.")

> **Please note:** You should not pronounce the letter sounds separately (e.g., /s/ and /a/). Instead, blend the two sounds together. Model this for the students, and encourage them to say the consonant and vowel as one unit (e.g., /sa/) to avoid the distortion of sounding words out letter by letter.

- Next, repeat the word, drawing out the sounds (e.g., "Our word is *saaaat*.") and ask the students to identify the last sound they hear in the word (e.g., "What is the last sound we hear in *sat*?")

- Ask the students to select the letter *t* from the top pocket and place it at the end of the word in the bottom pocket.

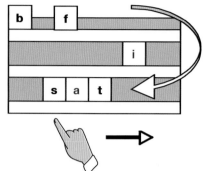

- Ask the students to read the whole word aloud. The students should move their pointer finger under the word from left to right while reading the word made on the sound board.

- Suggest ways to change the word (e.g., ask students to change *sat* to *sad*, then *sad* to *mad*).

> ***Please note:*** You can ask the whole group to construct a word together, or you can call on one student to take the lead. If one student is primarily responsible for constructing a given word, each student in the group also should construct the word on his or her sound board.

- Check each student's work, and provide corrective feedback. Remodel if necessary.

While the students are learning short vowels, it is best if you only change one sound at a time (e.g., change *mat* to *man*). When new vowels are introduced, *sat* easily becomes *sit*, then *sit* becomes *sip,* and then *ship.*

Use all of the consonant letters you have been reviewing with the students to make words with short /a/. As you introduce new consonants, add them to the sound board.

Once students have learned a new vowel sound (e.g., short /i/) in Step 1, introduce words with that vowel on the sound board. Include only five or six words in the sound board lesson, as shown in the sample sound board lists on the next page.

Sample Sound Board Lists

In the sample sound board lists provided, use only one list for each lesson.

Sample lists to use with short /a/ (read down):

at	sad	an	Al
rat	had	pan	pal
cat	ham	man	pad
cap	am	mat	mad
nap	as	fat	map
nab	has	at	lap

Sample lists to use with short /i/:

it	lid	Tim	pin
bit	hid	him	fin
big	his	hip	fit
pig	is	tip	hit
pit	in	tin	him
fit	pin	in	rim

Sample lists to use with short /a/ and /i/:

at	fit	rim	lap
hat	fin	ram	lip
ham	fan	am	tip
him	pan	Sam	tap
hit	pat	sat	tan
bit	pit	sit	tin
bat	it	sip	in

Sample lists to use with short /o/ and mixed vowel practice:

hot	top	tap	hop
hop	mop	top	hip
pop	mob	hop	rip
pot	sob	hot	rib
got	rob	rot	rob
rot	rod	rat	sob

Sample lists with short /u/ and mixed vowel practice:

cup	hug	cap	hum
cut	tug	cup	him
cub	tub	cop	rim
rub	rub	cot	rig
rug	run	hot	rug
hug	sun	hut	rag

Sample lists with short /e/ and mixed vowel practice:

fed	ten	dig	nut
led	pen	dug	net
let	pep	lug	pet
wet	pet	leg	pen
met	set	peg	pin
men	met	pig	tin

Once the five short vowel sounds and consonant sounds are learned, digraphs (*th, ch, sh,* and *-ck*) can be added to the closed syllable words that you introduce on the sound board.

Please note: Each digraph is written on a single card because the letters in a digraph combine to make one sound.

The two lists below provide some examples for practice reading words with digraphs.

Sample lists to use with digraphs (read down):

lip	sock
ship	sick
shop	sip
hop	chip
chop	ship
chip	shin
chin	thin

The Additional Materials section at the end of this level contains additional sample lists for the sound board.

Step 3

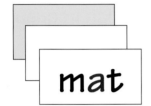

5 minutes

mat

Review Phonetically Regular Words (PRWs) and High Frequency Words (HFWs)

Materials

 Phonetically regular word (PRW) cards (only include those words you plan to use in a particular lesson)

 High frequency word (HFW) cards (only include those words you plan to use in a particular lesson)

Procedures

The goal of this activity is to develop fluency in reading individual words.

The focus is on phonetically regular words, with a few high frequency words included. Each student should have about two or three turns to read words. If you have a group of five students, for example, you might start off with about 15 words. At first, 12 words would be phonetically regular words and 3 would be high frequency words. As the students progress through the levels in this program, the number of words in this step will increase.

The phonetically regular words and high frequency words should not be written on the same color cards. We suggest white cards for phonetically regular words and yellow cards for high frequency words.

Phonetically Regular Words (PRWs)

- When students can make words with short /a/ on the sound board (Step 2), put words with short /a/ on your phonetically regular word (PRW) cards. Use these cards the same way the sound pack was used in Step 1.

- As words with each new short vowel sound are learned on the sound board (Step 2), add words with those vowels to the phonetically regular word cards.

- When students can make words with one of the digraphs (e.g., *sh* as in **ship**) on the sound board (Step 2), add words with that digraph to your phonetically regular word cards and introduce the next digraph(s) on the sound board (e.g., *ch* as in **chop**, *th* as in **thin**, and *-ck* as in *lock*).

- As words with each new digraph are learned on the sound board (Step 2), add words with those digraphs to the phonetically regular word cards.

The goal in Step 3 is for students to increase both accuracy and fluency in reading individual words. ***Students should have the opportunity to engage in repeated readings of the word cards.*** It is a good idea for students and/or teachers to keep a chart to monitor how long it takes the students to read a set number of words. Both the number of words and their complexity will increase as students move through the levels of this program.

A starter set of phonetically regular words (PRWs) is provided on the next page and on the CD-ROM ●. Lists of additional PRWs for each vowel sound are included in the Additional Materials section at the end of this level. You will need blank white cards so that you can add to the starter set as the students learn more words. As shown in the starter set, make sure to write the consonants in black and the vowels in red.

Starter Set of Red Level Phonetically Regular Word (PRW) Cards

_a_	**_i_**	**_o_**	**_u_**	**_e_**
sat	sip	rod	rub	set
mat	lip	got	tub	bet
fan	rid	dot	nut	fed
hat	tip	hot	run	web
pat	pit	pot	pup	pet
cap	fit	rob	cup	jet
pad	kid	cop	fun	red
pal	hid	top	cut	let
mad	did	not	rug	yes
tab			bus	ten

_th_	**_ch_**	**_sh_**	**_-ck_**
bath	chin	ship	back
thin	chip	shed	sick
thud	rich	cash	rock
	such	fish	duck
			neck

High Frequency Words (HFWs)

An Important Note About Teaching High Frequency Words

All of the high frequency words in this program are from *The Reading Teacher's Book of Lists* by Fry and Kress (2006). Fry and Kress refer to these words as "Instant Words." They have ranked the words in order of frequency of use in written material.

The first 300 words on Fry and Kress's (2006) Instant Word list are included in *Road to Reading* as high frequency words. Each level in the program includes 50 of the words from the Instant Word lists, but this number is just meant to be a guide.

You may find that the students already know most of the high frequency words in the Red Level. In this case, you can then introduce the high frequency words in the Orange Level while you continue to work on other Red Level skills.

If students have learned the decoding skills at the Red Level but do not know all of the high frequency words, you should move on to the Orange Level but continue to review the high frequency words from the Red Level.

There are many lists of high frequency words (e.g., Dolch words). The reading series that you use in your school may also have high frequency words that the students are required to learn. ***Feel free to substitute the high frequency word list of your choice for the one we have provided.***

Although students need to be fluent with many high frequency words, there is no prescribed order in which these words must be learned or absolute list of which words should be included.

High Frequency Words (HFWs) 1–50

The following high frequency words (HFWs) from Fry and Kress (2006) will be the first 50 words in your word card pack. You might want to pretest the students on these HFWs at this level and create an individualized list of HFWs that the students still need to learn. A High Frequency Word Assessment form for the Red Level and individual word cards are included on the CD-ROM.

the	of	*and	a	to	*in	*is
you	*that	*it	he	was	for	on
are	*as	*with	*his	they	I	*at
be	*this	have	from	or	one	*had
by	word	*but	*not	what	all	were
we	when	your	*can	said	there	use
*an	each	which	she	do	how	their
*if						

Adapted from *The Reading Teacher's Book of Lists, Fifth Edition,* by E.B. Fry and J. Kress
© 2006 Jossey-Bass. Reprinted with permission from John Wiley & Sons, Inc.

*Students will be learning to decode the words written in red at this level in this program. They are phonetically regular words.

Once each high frequency word has been learned by most of the students, it is a good idea to file the word in alphabetical order in the back of a high frequency word box. These words should be reviewed on a regular basis in Step 3 of your lesson to make sure that the students remember them.

Use any strategy you typically use to teach and review high frequency words (HFWs). Directions for four activities/games to add to your repertoire follow. Each of these games also can be played using only phonetically regular words (PRWs).

1. Complete the Sentence

2. "Go Fish"

3. Concentration

4. Board Game

1. Complete the Sentence

Materials

A dry erase board

HFW cards that will be used for the activity

A dry erase marker

To Play

- First, review with students the high frequency words (HFWs) that you will be asking them to use in the sentences.

- Write one simple sentence on the dry erase board for each student in your group. Use the name of one of your students in each sentence, leaving a blank in the sentence to be filled in with one of the HFWs (e.g., Sally can hop in ____ mud).

- Put the HFWs used in this lesson in random order on the table.

- Ask each student to find the sentence with his or her name and read it.

- Have the student select the HFW that completes the sentence. Then, ask the student and/or group to read the sentence again.

2. "Go Fish"

Materials

⦿ Four copies of **each** of the HFW cards that you will be using in the day's lesson

To Play

- First, review with the students the high frequency words (HFWs) that you will be using in the game.

- Mix the cards well and deal four cards, one at a time, to each student.

- Place the rest of the cards *face down* in the center of the table.

- Have the players fan their cards and hold them. (The students may need help with this step.)

- Have one student ask the student to his or her right for a card that will match one of those in his or her own hand (e.g., "Give me *is*, please").

- If the student has the requested card, it is given to the asking student. The asking student then places the card face up on top of the matching card and reads the word out loud. Play then passes to the next student.

- If the student does not have the requested card, he or she tells the asking student that he or she does not have the card, then says, "Go fish" (e.g., "I don't have *is*. Go fish.").

- The asking student then picks the top card from the stack of cards in the center of the table.

- If the student draws the card originally requested (e.g., *is*), the card is shown to the group. The student then places the card face up on top of the matching card and reads the word out loud.

- If the student draws a card that does not match, that card is added to his or her hand. Either way, play then passes to the next student.

- If a student runs out of cards by making pairs, the student draws another card from the deck and continues to play until all of the cards in the deck are used.

- Each student collects matched pairs of words, putting the pairs down in front of him or her.

- At the end of the game, the students count their pairs and read their words out loud before handing the cards back to you.

3. Concentration

Materials

◗ Two copies of **each** of the HFW cards that you want to reinforce in the day's lesson

To Play

- First, review with the students the high frequency words (HFWs) that you will be using in the game.

- Mix up the cards to make sure they are in random order, and place the cards face down in rows in front of the students.

- Have the students try to find matching pairs. The first player turns two cards face up, placing them in exactly the same spot they were in when they were face down.

- The student reads the words that have been turned over.

- If the two cards have the same word on them, the student removes those cards and holds on to them until the end of the game.

- If the cards do not have the same word, the student turns them face down in exactly the same spot, and the play passes to the next student.

- Remind the students to "concentrate" and try to remember where each card is because doing so will help them make a match.

- After all of the cards have been matched, each player takes a turn reading his or her words to the group.

4. Board Game

Materials

○ One or two copies of **each** of the HFW cards that you want to reinforce in the day's lesson

A generic game board

One token for each student

One spinner

To Play

- First, review with the students the high frequency words (HFWs) that you will be using in the game. Mix up the HFWs, and place them face down in a pile on the table.

- Give each student a token to mark his or her space on the game board.

- The first student spins and picks a card.

- If the student reads the card correctly, he or she can move his or her token the number of spaces indicated on the spinner.

- If the student reads the word incorrectly, read the word, have the student repeat it correctly, and put the word at the bottom of the pile.

- Play until one student gets to the end of the game board (or until all students reach the end, if you have enough time in your lesson).

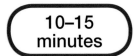

Step 4 Read Orally in Context

10–15 minutes

Materials

Selected decodable readers (see Red Level chart)

Selected books and/or stories from your classroom or school library or basal program (suggested book titles appear in Appendix B)

Procedures

You will be using a variety of books for oral reading. The books you choose should allow the students to practice the skills they have learned in the Red Level and to reinforce the importance of **accurate** and **fluent** reading as a foundation for comprehension.

In particular, we recommend including decodable books from several series, such as the following:

- Primary Phonics

- Bob Books

- Steck-Vaughn Phonics Readers

- Dr. Maggie's Phonics Readers

Although we list a variety of options for oral reading material, the choices you make will depend on the skill level of your students and the books that are available to you. ***You do not need to use the series that we have recommended.*** A variety of materials exist that reinforce the same skills that the students are learning in the Red Level, and you should feel free to substitute books from other series as appropriate.

Groups Moving Quickly

Groups who are moving quickly may spend less time reading decodable books in this level than groups who need more practice on short vowels in simple closed syllable words (e.g., *mat*).

Groups Needing More Practice

Groups needing more practice will spend considerably more time reading and rereading *more* decodable books as well as other available beginning readers.

Decodable Book Chart for the Red Level

To help you select books for your groups, we have created decodable book charts for the first five levels of this program.

The charts integrate books from a variety of **decodable readers**. Books on the Red Level chart are arranged by the vowels being reinforced.

> This chart is meant to help you individualize instruction for your students. **Remember, other decodable books may be substituted for those on the chart.**

The chart includes decodable books from Bob Books; Primary Phonics, Set 1; Dr. Maggie's Phonics Readers; and Steck-Vaughn Phonics Readers. We have integrated readers from these four series. The books that reinforce the short vowel sound /a/ are the first books on the chart.

> Although these books are highly decodable (phonetically regular), each book also introduces a small number of high frequency words; these words are also included on the chart.

Groups Moving Quickly

As stated previously, a group that is moving quickly might read only a few decodable readers that reinforce all five of the short vowels.

Groups Needing More Practice

A group that needs extended practice might need to read several decodable books that reinforce just one short vowel sound before moving on to additional short vowels. The number of books needed will depend on the accuracy and fluency of the students.

Red Level Decodable Book Chart

BB A = Bob Books Level A   DM = Dr. Maggie's Phonics Readers
SV = Steck-Vaughn   PP = Primary Phonics

		Title	Vowels	New Words*	Ending
Decodable Books with Short /a/					
1	BB A1-1	Mat	a	on	
2	BB A1-2	Sam	a	and, on, O.K.	
3	SV 1-1	Matt and Rags	a	is, a, and, the	-s
4	SV 1-2	Pam's Pal	a	a, is, on, and	-s, 's
5	DM-1	I Spy	a	spy, a, and, I, in, no, on, the, oh, scat	
6	PP 1-1	Mac and Tab	a	is, a, the, on, in, to, for, are	-s
7	DM-2	Hap and Cap	a	but, have, here, of, said, to, was, fast	
Decodable Books with Short /i/ (Includes Short /a/)					
		Title	Vowels	New Words*	Ending
8	BB A1-7	Jig and Mag	a, i	and, a	
9	SV 1-3	What Is It?	a, i	what, fill	
10	SV 1-4	Kiss a Pig	a, i	a, the, to, on, and, kiss, miss	-s
11	PP 1-2	The Tin Man	a, i	a, the, on, to, and, for, yellow, was	
Decodable Books with Short /o/ (Includes Short /a / and /i/)					
		Title	Vowels	New Words*	Ending
12	BB A1-3	Dot	a, o	a, the	
13	BB A 1-4	Mac	a, o	a, and, the	
14	BB A1-5	Dot and Mit	a, i, o	and, a	
15	BB A1-6	Dot and the Dog	a, i, o	and, a, the	

16	SV 1-7	Tom and His Mom	a, i, o	the, to, on, will, miss	
17	PP 1-3	Al	a, i, o	a, the, to, and, of, was	
18	DM-3	Top Job, Mom	a, i, o	new, said, so, put, the, blew, and, oh, no, uh, stop, cool	

Decodable Books with Short /u/ (Includes Short /a/, /i/, and /o/)					
		Title	**Vowels**	**New Words***	**Ending**
19	SV 1-5	Zig-Zag, Buzz and Hum	a, i, u	and, a, for, the, buzz	-s
20	BB A1-8	Muff and Ruff	a, i, o, u	and, a, to	
21	BB A1-9	10 Cut-Ups	a, i, o, u	Ruff, Muff	-s
22	SV 1-6	Fun in the Sun	a, i, o, u	a, and, the, have, are, will, hill, huffs, puffs	-s, 's
23	SV 1-8	Bob Has a Job	a, i, o, u	a, the, of, to, have, with, toss	-s
24	PP 1-4	Tim	a, i, o, u	a, the, to, and, or, was	

Decodable Books with Short /e/ (Includes Short /a/, /i/, /o/, and /u/)					
		Title	**Vowels**	**New Words***	**Ending**
25	BB A1-10	Peg and Ted	a, i, u, e	and, a, the, pink, went	
26	BB A1-11	Lad and the Fat Cat	a, i, o, u, e	and, the, a	-s
27	BB A1-12	The Vet	a, i, o, u, e	a, the, into, zoo, to, O.K.	
28	SV 1-9	Ten Hens	a, i, o, u, e	a, to, for, out, of, the, yell	-s
29	PP 1-5	The Jet	a, i, o, u, e	a, the, to, of, for, are, no, go	

Decodable Books with Short /e/ (Includes Short /a/, /i/, /o/, and /u/)					
		Title	**Vowels**	**New Words***	**Ending**
30	PP 1-6	Ben Bug	a, i, o, u, e	a, the, to, and, of, was	
31	PP 1-7	Ed	a, i, o, u, e	a, the, to, and, of, was	-s
32	PP 1-8	Meg	a, i, o, u, e	a, the, to, and, of, was	
33	PP 1-9	Ted	a, i, o, u, e	a, the, to, and, of, he	
34	PP 1-10	The Wig	a, i, o, u, e	a, the, to, and, of, was	
35	DM-4	Pom Pom's Big Win	a, i, o, e	today, day, puts, the, and, toy, spins, blue, ribbon, grin	-s, 's

*The *New Words* category in the decodable book chart includes both high frequency words that are being taught at this level and high frequency words that are not taught until later levels in the program. The *New Words* category also includes phonetically regular words with patterns that will be taught in later levels.

An Important Note About Building Fluency

To build fluency, it is necessary to include ***frequent repeated readings*** of text and to provide corrective feedback to the students. Students may need to read some of the beginning readers several times to begin to increase fluency. It has been our experience that some students will need to reread books from the Red Level when they are in the Orange Level before becoming fluent.

Additional opportunities for repeated reading can occur by putting completed books in a center where students can reread them at other times during the day. This should not, however, replace repeated reading with corrective feedback by the teacher because repeated reading with corrective feedback has been found to be the most effective method for developing fluency.

An Important Note About Selecting Books

In addition to reading decodable books, students at this level should also have opportunities for supported reading using popular trade books (e.g., easy reading children's books).

At first, you may be doing most of the reading. As students become more proficient, they will be reading more of the text.

Appendix B contains some titles of trade books that students, with support, can successfully read. ***Again, feel free to substitute your favorite books for students reading at this beginning level.***

Step 5 Dictation

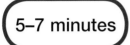

5–7 minutes

Materials

Refer to Dry Erase Board Dictation (p. 48) and Notebook Dictation (p. 54) for materials.

This step includes descriptions of two different versions of the daily dictation activity–*dry erase board dictation* and *notebook dictation.*

Some students, particularly those who are not yet proficient with paper and pencil tasks, may need to start with *dry erase board dictation.* When these students are ready to transition to pencil and paper dictation, follow the directions for *notebook dictation*.

Most students will be using notebooks for *notebook dictation* from the first lesson in the Red Level. These notebooks can be used as a record of each student's spelling progress throughout this program.

Dry Erase Board Dictation

Materials

One dry erase board, one dry erase marker, and one eraser for each student and teacher

One alphabet strip for each student (as needed, for students who cannot yet write all of the letters from memory)

Procedures

- Give each student a dry erase board, a marker, an eraser, and, if needed, an alphabet strip.

- Tell the students, "Today, you are going to write words you already know how to spell!" (If using the alphabet strips, also say, "You can use the alphabet strips to help you remember how to make the letters.")

- Demonstrate on a dry erase board so that the students know what you want them to do.

- First, say the word **at**. Then, say it again slowly—**aaaaaaat**.

- Ask the students how many sounds they hear. Then, ask them how many letters they think you should write.

- Write the word on the dry erase board as you say it again slowly.

- Now, tell the students to write the word *at*.

- Tell the students to say the word slowly and listen for all the sounds as they write the word.

- Check each student's work and help him or her to correct the word if you see an error (e.g., if a student writes *it* instead of *at*, say, "You wrote *it*. I wanted you to write ***aaaat***. Show me how you would change ***iiiit*** to ***aaaat***").

- When you are pronouncing the words, remember to stretch out the sounds.

- If the students continue to have difficulty, demonstrate again for the students on your dry erase board, and move on to the next word.

- When you dictate the next word, remind the students to say the word slowly and listen for all the sounds.

- When you dictate a proper noun, such as the word *Sam*, remind the students to use a capital letter at the beginning because *Sam* is a name.

Eight Ways to Individualize Dictation within Groups

1. Have the student write only the first sound or last sound.

2. Have the student copy the word from your dry erase board.

3. Put blank lines on the dry erase board prior to dictation, and fill in the vowel for the student. Have the student fill in the first or the last sound or both.

4. Designate one student as the Word Repeater or Echo. This student repeats the word after you dictate it and reads the word after students have written it on their dry erase boards.

5. If a student needs a model, point to the letters on the alphabet strip or have him or her trace the word that you have written on the dry erase board.

6. Make generic spelling booklets using four laminated sheets (or just plain sheets) of paper. Each sheet should have three boxes ☐☐☐ or three blanks ___ ___ ___. Fill in the correct vowel for each word prior to dictating the words. Cross out one blank on the page if only two blanks are needed (e.g., *at*). These books can be used by all students on any given day.

7. On the student's dry erase board, write the letter that the dictated word starts with using dots. Have the student connect the dots.

8. If a student has difficulty with fine motor skills, write all of the words that are being dictated that day on the student's dry erase board. Then, ask the student to point to and trace the word being dictated.

Sample Lists for Dry Erase Board Dictation

Below and on the next two pages are sample lists that can be used for the dry erase board dictation. Each of the sample lists contains only four words. Feel free to increase the number of words dictated if your students are successful with the first four. The first lists contain only words with short /a/.

> Do not introduce a new vowel until your students can make words with that vowel on the sound board in Step 2.

For some groups, you will need to generate additional dry erase board lists using only short /a/ words because the students will need more practice before moving on to spelling words with short /i/. If some groups do not know all of their consonants yet, generate lists that use only the consonants they know. You could also write the word, perhaps leaving out just the initial or final consonant, for an individual student who needs more assistance.

Sample lists to use with short /a/:

1. at, pat, Sam, pan

2. at, mat, map, tap

3. an, ran, rat, sat

4. tan, lap, hat, mad

5. sad, tap, at, wag

<u>Sample lists to use with short /i/ and /a/:</u>

When your students can make words with short /i/ on the sound board, add short /i/ words to dictation.

1. it, sit, fit, fin

2. at, sat, sit, sip

3. it, fit, rat, rip

4. cap, zip, lid, fin

<u>Sample lists to use with short /o/, /i/, and /a/:</u>

When your students can make words with short /o/ on the sound board, add short /o/ words to dictation.

1. top, mom, pot, rod

2. dot, map, job, sat

3. hot, tin, hop, pin

4. lap, him, mop, top

Sample lists to use with short /u/, /o/, /i/, and /a/:

When your students can make words with short /u/ on the sound board, add short /u/ words to dictation.

1.   up, hug, cup, rub

2.   run, up, fun, nut

3.   mud, ham, win, sun

4.   top, hut, bug, lip

Sample lists to use with short /e/, /u/, /o/, /i/, and /a/:

When your students can make words with short /e/ on the sound board, add short /e/ words to dictation.

1.   red, ten, pet, fed

2.   pet, sad, mop, net

3.   up, fed, men, top

4.   hug, red, hen, up

Notebook Dictation

Materials

Dictation notebook for each student

Pencil

One dry erase board, dry erase marker, and eraser for the teacher for demonstration

Procedures

- Each dictation exercise should include four or five words and one short sentence (four to five words) that uses words with the same phonetic pattern.

- Prior to the first dictation lesson in which the students will be using a dictation notebook, demonstrate on your dry erase board how students should set up their notebook pages.

- At the beginning of each notebook dictation session, ask the students to put the date on the top of that day's page. This provides an informal method of monitoring each student's day-to-day spelling progress.

- Tell the students what vowels you will be using for that day's lesson. These vowels will be their column headings.

- Have the students write the vowel headings on their page to help organize the dictation.

- Have the students write each word under the appropriate vowel as the word is dictated.

Example of notebook dictation pages:

<table>
<tr><td><u>a</u></td><td><u>i</u></td></tr>
<tr><td>mat</td><td>him</td></tr>
<tr><td>rag</td><td>fin</td></tr>
<tr><td></td><td>sit</td></tr>
</table>

The rat can sit.

<table>
<tr><td><u>a</u></td><td><u>i</u></td><td><u>u</u></td><td><u>e</u></td></tr>
<tr><td>at</td><td>him</td><td>pup</td><td>pet</td></tr>
<tr><td></td><td>bit</td><td></td><td></td></tr>
</table>

The pup bit him.

- Check each student's work and help him or her correct the word if you see an error (e.g., "If a student writes *it* instead of *at*, say, "You wrote *it*. I wanted you to write ***aaaat***. Show me how you would change ***iiiit*** to ***aaaat***.").

- When you are pronouncing the words, remember to stretch out the sounds.

- If the student continues to have difficulty, demonstrate for the student on *your* dry erase board, then move on to the next word.

- When you dictate the next word, tell the students to say the word slowly and listen for all of the sounds.

- After you dictate the individual words, dictate one short sentence (as shown in the sample dication pages above).

- Tell the students to write the sentence on a separate line.

- If needed, help the students spell any words in the sentence that can't be sounded out (e.g., *the*).

- At the end of the dictation lesson, have the students read orally all of the words they have written under the vowel headings and also read the sentence.

> ***Please note:*** The ***dictated sentence*** should include words with the same phonetic patterns being practiced in that day's dictation. You do not need to use the exact words that were dictated. It is more challenging if you use different words. The composition of the sentence and whether it includes any of the dictated words will vary depending on the needs of the group.
>
> Remember, help the students spell any word in the sentence that can't be sounded out (e.g., *the*).

Once students can make words with digraphs (e.g., /sh/ as in __ship__) on the sound board and you have included the digraphs in other steps of the lesson, you are ready to include words with digraphs in dictation.

<u>Example of notebook dictation page with digraphs:</u>

a	***i***	***u***
bath	chin	shut
sack	fish	

Ben has a hot bath.

Also refer to the Additional Materials section at the end of this level for more sample dictation exercises and additional phonetically regular words that can be used for dictation.

Additional Materials

Red Level

Phonetically Regular Word Lists (*a* and *i*)

a			*i*	
at	dad		in	fig
pat	rag		did	kid
cab	sad		pin	lit
tap	lap		rip	dig
Al	had		rib	six
mat	zap		tin	fix
cap	fax		lip	zip
cat	wag		lid	mix
pal	max		big	win
fat	wax		pig	wig
map	nap		hid	Tim
bat	bad		fin	sit
ham	fan		kit	pit

Red Level

Phonetically Regular Word Lists (*o* and *u*)

o		*u*	
Bob	rot	up	cub
mom	pop	cut	rug
lot	jog	mug	bum
cop	top	nut	jug
rob	hot	tub	dug
mop	nod	run	cup
sob	not	sun	gum
Tom	ox	mud	bug
got	job	hut	bun
mob	pod	pup	hug
pot	box	fun	rub
fox	hop	us	yum

Red Level

Phonetically Regular Word Lists (e)

e	
bed	fed
men	hem
bet	net
red	Ted
beg	pen
set	leg
ten	met
pet	wet
peg	yet
let	Ned
den	get
led	pep
web	hen

Red Level

Phonetically Regular Word Lists (*th, ch,* and *sh*)

th	*ch*	*sh*	
that	chip	ship	hush
thin	chat	shop	cash
thud	chop	shed	fish
bath	rich	shut	mash
path	much	rush	gush
math	chin	dash	
them	chug	wish	
Beth	such		
Seth			

Red Level

Phonetically Regular Word Lists (-*ck*)

a	*i*	*o*	*u*	*e*
back	Dick	dock	duck	deck
pack	Nick	lock	luck	neck
lack	kick	jock	muck	peck
Jack	lick	rock	puck	check
rack	pick	sock	tuck	
sack	sick		yuck	
tack	Rick		shuck	
shack	wick			
quack	chick			
	thick			
	quick			

Red Level

Sample Sound Board Exercises

a

1. at – rat – cat – cap – nap – nab – tab
2. sad – had – ham – hat – mat – man – ran
3. an – pan – man – mat – fat – bat – bad
4. pad – mad – map – lap – rap – rat – at
5. nap – tap – tan – pan – fan – fat – sat
6. an – man – pan – pad – had – sad – dad
7. map – mad – sad – sat – hat – ham – ram
8. man – can – ran – rap – gap – lap – tap

Red Level

Sample Sound Board Exercises

i

1. it – bit – big – pig – pit – fit – lit
2. sit – sip – lip – lid – hid – hip – dip
3. pin – pig – dig – wig – win – tin – tip
4. hip – tip – tin – fin – fit – kit – kid
5. tip – lip – lid – rid – rim – dim – dig
6. in – pin – pit – fit – bit – big – rig
7. pin – in – tin – tip – sip – sit – it
8. kid – rid – rib – bib – bit – fit – pit

Red Level

Sample Sound Board Exercises

a and i

1. at – hat – ham – him – hit – sit – sat
2. at – sat – sit – pit – pat – rat – rap
3. rim – him – hit – hat – at – it – sit
4. pin – pan – an – tan – tap – tip – lip
5. fit – fin – fan – pan – pat – pit – it
6. am – at – sat – sit – sip – lip – lap
7. sap – map – man – tan – tin – pin – pit
8. in – win – wig – wag – sag – bag – big
9. sat – bat – bag – big – wig – wag – rag
10. rap – rip – lip – lap – sap – sip – tip

Red Level

Sample Sound Board Exercises

o with a and i

1. hit – hot – hop – pop – pot – got – dot
2. tip – top – mop – mob – sob – rob – rot
3. box – bob – bog – jog – job – rob – rot
4. top – tom – mom – mop – cop – cot – cat
5. top – tap – rap – rip – rib – rob – sob
6. rot – hot – hop – hip – tip – rip – rib
7. cot – hot – hat – rat – rot – rob – sob
8. bag – bat – bit – sit – fit – fib – bib
9. sad – lad – lid – lit – lot – cot – cat
10. hat – pat – pit – pot – dot – lot – lit

Red Level

Sample Sound Board Exercises

u with a, i, and o

1. cup – cub – cut – but – bug – bud – bus
2. hug – tug – tub – rub – run – sun – fun
3. mud – mug – rug – tug – tub – cub – rub
4. fun – run – rug – bug – bum – gum – hum
5. bun – but – bug – hug – hut – nut – cut
6. bug – rug – rag – tag – tug – jug – mug
7. run – ran – ban – bun – fun – fan – fin
8. sum – hum – him – ham – hat – mat – sat
9. up – cup – cap – cop – top – tip – tap
10. hum – him – rim – rib – rub – sub – cub

Red Level

Sample Sound Board Exercises

e with i, o, and u

1. met – men – ten – pen – pet – set – wet

2. get – set – pet – pen – den – hen – hem

3. hen – ten – pen – pet – pit – lit – let

4. ten – pen – pet – pot – hot – hop – hip

5. got – get – bet – let – set – sit – lit

6. web – wet – net – not – nod – rod – red

7. leg – peg – pig – rig – rip – rap – lap

8. lot – let – led – lid – hid – him – hum

9. pot – pet – set – sat – at – am – ram

10. red – rid – lid – led – let – lit – kit

Red Level

Sample Sound Board Exercises

th, sh, ch, and -ck with a, i, o, u, and e

1. shop – shot – shut – hut – hush – rush – rash
2. at – that – bat – bath – path – pan – pen
3. lip – ship – shop – hop – chop – chip – chin
4. bath – math – map – sap – sash – mash – mush
5. rash – rush – rug – mug – much – mud – thud
6. deck – duck – luck – lock – shock – shack – tack
7. shut – shot – shock – sock – sack – sick – lick
8. shock – tock – tick – chick – check – neck – net
9. duck – dock – dot – pot – pat – pack – quack
10. pen – then – them – hem – ham – hash – rash
11. back – pack – peck – deck – check – chick – chin
12. duck – deck – check – chick – chin – thin – win
13. such – much – muck – tuck – tick – sick – sock
14. tin – chin – thin – thick – kick – lick – luck
15. tack – quack – quick – quit – hit – hut – hush
16. quiz – quit – quick – thick – thin – chin – shin
17. sick – quick – pick – pit – quit – lit – lick

Red Level

Sample Dictation Exercises

a and i

a	***i***
man	tin
sad	kid

The cat is mad.

a	***i***
pal	sit
mad	him

The tin man is sad.

a, i, and o

a	***i***	***o***
rag	big	mop
	pit	hot

Tom got a job.

a	***i***	***o***
sad	bit	job
	Tim	not

The rag is on the cot.

Red Level

Sample Dictation Exercises

a, i, and u

_a_	**_i_**	**_u_**
map	pig	mud
	lid	up

The pup is in the mud.

a, o, and u

_a_	**_o_**	**_u_**
fan	hot	rug
nap		sun

It is fun to nap.

Red Level

Sample Dictation Exercises

th

_a_	_i_
path	thin
that	tip

That man is his dad.

_a_	_i_
bath	win
math	with

Ben got in the bath.

ch

_u_	_i_
much	chin
run	rich

He is a rich man.

_u_	_i_
fun	chick
such	chip

Chuck had a chip.

Red Level

Sample Dictation Exercises

sh

i	*o*	*u*
fish	pot	shut
	shop	

Ted had a hot fish.

a	*u*	*e*
cap	hush	shed
dash		

I will shut up the shed.

-ck

a	*i*	*u*
tack	kick	hut
		Chuck

Chuck sat on the tack.

a	*i*	*u*
shack	Rick	luck
sat		

Did Chuck kick the dog?

Orange Level

Skills to Review

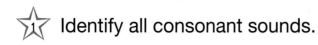 Identify all consonant sounds.

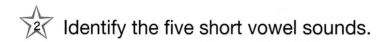 Identify the five short vowel sounds.

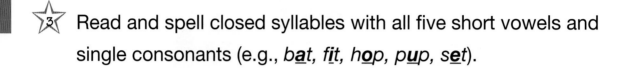 Read and spell closed syllables with all five short vowels and single consonants (e.g., b<u>a</u>t, f<u>i</u>t, h<u>o</u>p, p<u>u</u>p, s<u>e</u>t).

 Identify the digraphs *th, ch, sh,* and *-ck.*

⭐ Read and spell closed syllable words with the digraphs *th, ch, sh,* and *-ck* (e.g., **th<u>i</u>ck, sh<u>i</u>n, ch<u>i</u>ck**).

Goals for the Orange Level

When the students complete this level, they should be able to do the following:

⭐1 Read and spell closed syllables with double final consonants -*ll*, -*ss*, and -*ff* (e.g., we**ll**, mi**ss**, pu**ff**).

⭐2 Read and spell closed syllables with initial *l* blends (*bl, cl, fl, gl, sl, pl*), *r* blends (*cr, dr, gr, br, fr, pr, tr*), *s* blends (*sk, sm, sn, sp, st, sw*), and *tw*.

⭐3 Read and spell closed syllables with final blends (-*mp, -sk, -st, -ft, -lt, -nt, -lf, -lp, -nd,* and *-nk*).

⭐4 Read and spell closed syllable words with -*s* and -*ing* when there is no change to the spelling of the base word (e.g., hat**s**, jump**s**, rock**ing**, fish**ing**).

> ***Please note:*** If students are both accurate and fluent with one-syllable words (closed syllables) at this level, you might want to introduce the compound words made up of only closed syllables (e.g., *sunset, bathtub*) that can be found in the Additional Materials at the end of the Yellow Level.

An Important Reminder About Teaching High Frequency Words

Assigning high frequency words to a particular level in the program is arbitrary. Once the students can read closed syllables with blends in the initial and final position, they are ready to go on to the Yellow Level, in which they will learn to read final "e" syllables. If your students have not learned all of the high frequency words in the Orange Level, you can continue to work on the high frequency words introduced in this level as you teach the new decoding skills in the Yellow Level. ***Mastery of high frequency words is not necessary to progress to the next level.***

Although all students progress at different rates in learning to read both phonetically regular words and high frequency words, some groups will need to be introduced to high frequency words *much more slowly* than others. Once students have a solid foundation of decoding skills, they tend to learn the high frequency words more quickly.

Step 1

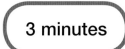

(3 minutes)

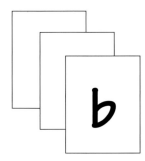

Review Sound–Symbol Correspondences

Materials

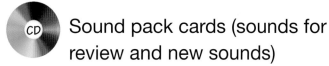 Sound pack cards (sounds for review and new sounds)

Step

1

Procedures

Use your sound pack of previously learned letters to quickly review the letter names and sounds with your students. Remember, the goal is to develop fluency, not boredom.

Once mastery of consonants, digraphs, and *all* short vowels has been reached, vary the consonants and digraphs that you review each day. **You should, however, continue to review all of the short vowels at the beginning of every lesson.**

- Remember, for the short vowels, ask the student for the name, sound, and *key word* (e.g., *a* says /a/ as in **a**pple, *i* says /i/ as in **i**tch, *o* says /o/ as in **o**ctopus, *u* says /u/ as in **u**p, *e* says /e/ as in **E**d.)

Step 1

> ***Please note: Blends (e.g., br, fl, sk) are not put on one card, and they are not introduced in Step 1 of the lesson.*** Because each letter of the blend retains its own sound, learning blends requires that the students put together individual sounds that they already know.
>
> Blends are hard to pronounce in isolation. Consequently, we introduce the concept of blends on the sound board in Step 2 of the Five-Step Plan, and each letter of the blend will remain on a separate card.

Step 2

Teach or Review New Decoding Skill

5–7 minutes

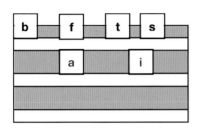

Materials

 Sound board for each student

 Consonant letters and digraphs in the top pocket (only include those needed to make words for a particular lesson)

 Vowel letters in the middle pocket (only include those needed to make words for a particular lesson)

Procedures

Once the five short vowel sounds, consonant sounds, and digraphs are mastered, double final consonants and initial and final blends will be added to the closed syllable words that you introduce on the sound board.

Double Final Consonants

You will be using the sound board to introduce closed syllable words with double final consonants *-ll*, *-ss*, and *-ff* (e.g., we**ll**, me**ss**, pu**ff**). ***(Make sure you have two copies of the letters l, s, and f to use on the sound board.)*** The three lists below give you some examples to use on the sound board to introduce double final letters. Later, words with double final letters will be interspersed in lists with blends.

> Remind the students that you only double the final consonant when the word ends in *l*, *s,* or *f.*

Sample lists to use with double final consonants (read down):

tell	mess	hat
fell	mass	hut
fill	pass	huff*
bill	pat	buff*
hill	bat	cuff
chill	bass*	cut

> *Do the students know what the words ***huff*** and ***buff*** mean?
>
> Look for other opportunities to extend vocabulary in each lesson.

> *Do the students know what a ***bass*** is?
>
> If not, this is a good opportunity to expand vocabulary.

Blends

The order in which blends are introduced is arbitrary and varies from program to program. We chose to use the order for the introduction of blends that is used in *Explode the Code 2* (Hall & Price, 2002).

Feel free to use a different sequence to introduce blends and to adapt the lists we have provided to reflect the sequence you are using.

Remember, unlike digraphs, blends are *not* written on a single card. In a blend, each letter retains its individual sound. Thus, the students should be able to select the two (or, later, three) cards that are needed for each blend.

- First, introduce the blends *bl, cl, fl,* and *gl* on the sound board.

- Next, have the students make the word *fat* on the sound board and then change *fat* to *flat*.

- Then, put the consonant letters back in the top pocket and the vowel in the middle pocket and start over, turning *cap* into *clap*.

- Follow this procedure several more times using the pairs on the next page.

Sample pairs (read across):

lip	------------------------------►	flip
lap	------------------------------►	clap
lock	------------------------------►	block
back	------------------------------►	black
gum	------------------------------►	glum
lot	------------------------------►	blot

Once the students can make the **pairs** with the blends, you can go back to making **lists** and changing only one sound at a time.

Sample lists to use with blends *bl, cl, fl,* and *gl* (read down):

lap	cap	lip	back
clap	clap	flip	black
clip	flap	clip	sack
lip	lap	lip	Sam
ship	lip	lit	sum
shop	flip	lot	gum
▼ shock	▼ flick	▼ blot	▼ glum

The order for the introduction of blends is listed below (Hall & Price, 2002).

<u>Initial blends:</u>

1. *bl,*   *cl,*   *fl,*   *gl*

2. *sk,*   *sl,*   *pl*

3. *cr,*   *dr,*   *gr*

4. *br,*   *fr,*   *pr,*   *tr*

5. *sm,*   *sn,*   *sp*

6. *st,*   *sw,*   *tw*

<u>Final blends:</u>

7. *-mp,*   *-sk,*   *-st*

8. *-ft,*   *-lt,*   *-nt*

9. *-lf,*   *-lp,*   *-nd,*   *-nk*

To help you create lists for the sound board, select words from the word lists in the Additional Materials section at the end of this level. The Additional Materials section also contains sample sound board exercises that reinforce the blends that have been introduced.

Step

2

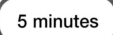

Step 3

5 minutes

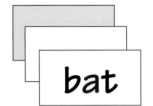

bat

Review Phonetically Regular Words (PRWs) and High Frequency Words (HFWs)

Materials

Phonetically regular word (PRW) cards (only include those words you plan to use in a particular lesson)

High frequency word (HFW) cards (only include those words you plan to use in a particular lesson)

Procedures

The goal of this activity is to develop fluency. The focus is on phonetically regular words, with a few high frequency words included. Each student should have about three turns to read words. If you have a group of five students, for example, you might start off with about 15 words. At first, 12 words would be phonetically regular words and 3 would be high frequency words.

As the students progress through the levels in this program, the number of words in this step will increase. You might include, for example, 15 phonetically regular words and 5 high frequency words.

> As with the Red Level, the phonetically regular words (PRWs) and high frequency words (HFWs) should not be written on the same color cards.

Phonetically Regular Words (PRWs)

Closed Syllable Words with Double Final Consonants

Once the students can successfully make words with double final consonants (*-ll*, *-ss*, and *-ff*) on the sound board, you can add that group of words to your phonetically regular word (PRW) cards.

Closed Syllable Words with Blends

Once the students can successfully make words with the first set of blends (*bl, cl, fl,* and *gl*) on the sound board, you can add that group of words to your phonetically regular word (PRW) cards and introduce the next set of blends (*sk, sl,* and *sp*) on the sound board.

A starter set of PRWs is provided on the next page and on the CD-ROM ⊙. As shown in the starter set, make sure to write the consonants in black and the vowels in red.

Starter Set of Orange Level Phonetically Regular Word (PRW) Cards

Double final consonants

_-ll_	**_-ss_**	**_-ff_**
fill	miss	cliff
well	mess	stiff
chill	pass	sniff
hill	kiss	Jeff
		puff

Initial blends

_bl_	**_cl_**	**_fl_**	**_gl_**
block	clam	flag	glad
blab	class	flush	glass
blush	clock	flip	glob
	club		

_sk_	**_sl_**	**_pl_**
skim	slam	plum
skip	sled	plan
skill	slug	plop
	slush	

_cr_	**_dr_**	**_gr_**
crab	drop	grill
crib	drum	grab
crash	drip	grin

Step
3

Initial blends (*continued*)

br	**fr**	**pr**	**tr**
brat	fresh	press	trip
brass	Fran	prop*	truck
brick	frill*		trap

sm	**sn**	**sp**	
smell	snap	spell	speck*
smock*	snack	spin	spill
smack	snob*	spot	spit

st	**sw**	**tw**
stash*	swim	twin
step	swell	twig
stop	swish*	
stick		

*Do your students know the meanings of the words with asterisks?

If not, this is a good opportunity to expand vocabulary.

Final blends

-mp	**-sk**	**-st**
camp	ask	fast
champ	desk	nest
dump	risk	must

Starter Set of Orange Level PRW Cards (*continued*)

Final blends (*continued*)

-ft	**-lt**	**-nt**
raft*	belt	ant
gift	melt	sent
lift	tilt*	mint
		went

-lf	**-lp**	**-nd**	**-nk**
elf	help	and	sink
shelf	gulp*	hand	dunk
		send	chunk
		pond	

*Do your students know the meanings of the words with asterisks?

If not, this is a good opportunity to expand vocabulary.

Closed Syllable Words with -s and -ing

In this step you will also introduce the endings -s and -ing to closed syllable words when there is no change to the spelling of the base word (e.g., hat**s**, jump**s**, rock**ing**, fish**ing**).

As students become accurate and fluent reading closed syllable words with single consonants, digraphs, and blends, you can add words with -s and -ing to your phonetically regular word (PRW) cards.

Additional sample lists of phonetically regular words with final double consonants and blends taught in this level are included in the Additional Materials section at the end of this level.

High Frequency Words (HFWs) 51–100

The following high frequency words (HFWs) from Fry and Kress (2006) can be taught and added to your word card pack. You might want to pretest the students on these HFWs at this level and create an individualized list of HFWs that the students still need to learn. A High Frequency Word Assessment form for the Orange Level and individual word cards are included on the CD-ROM.

**will	*up	other	about	out	many	*then
*them	these	so	some	her	would	make
like	*him	into	time	*has	look	two
more	write	go	see	number	no	way
could	people	my	*than	first	water	been
call	who	*am	**its	now	find	long
down	day	*did	*get	come	made	may
part						

Adapted from *The Reading Teacher's Book of Lists, Fifth Edition,* by E.B. Fry and J. Kress
© 2006 Jossey-Bass. Reprinted with permission from John Wiley & Sons, Inc.

*Students learned to decode words written in red during the Red Level in this program.

**Students will be learning to decode the words written in orange at this level in this program.

Once each high frequency word has been learned by most of the students, it is a good idea to file the word in alphabetical order in the back of a high frequency word box. These words should be reviewed on a regular basis in Step 3 of your lesson to make sure that the students remember them.

Use any strategy you typically use to teach high frequency words (HFWs). Review the suggestions in the Red Level, including playing "Go Fish," Concentration, and the Board Game to reinforce these high frequency words.

An Important Note About Developing Fluency

Remember, the overall goal of this activity is to develop fluency at the word level. A hallmark of good readers is the ability to read both accurately and fluently. Students will start to develop fluency at the word level during Step 3. To help students develop fluency, you will need to have them read the words more than once.

- The first time the words are read, the goal is accuracy.

- If a student misreads a vowel in a word (reading *slip* for *slap*), it helps to point to the vowel and ask the student to tell you the sound the vowel makes (e.g., *a* says /a/).

- Next, point to the first letters of the word and slide your finger from left to right, asking the student to blend the consonant(s) and vowel (e.g., *slaaaaaaap*).

- Finally, ask the student to read the entire word (e.g., *slap*).

- If the student continues to read the word incorrectly, then pronounce the word for the student and move on. Place that word on the bottom of the pack of cards, and try to give the same student the opportunity to read that word at his or her next turn.

Activities for Developing Fluency

- When the students read the words for the second time, try using an hourglass to encourage the students to move more quickly. The students like to see how many words they can read before the sand runs out.

- Use a stopwatch with the group and have the students see how long it takes to read all of the words in the card pack for that day. As you go around the group, you can accommodate a student who reads less fluently by asking that student to read a word that you know he or she can read. This ensures that each student gets a turn and keeps the activity moving.

- Students can also use the hourglass and stopwatch while working in pairs. Each student tries to read his or her words more quickly than during his or her previous reading. This way, the students are encouraged to improve their own times and not compete with each other.

Step 4 Read Orally in Context

10–15 minutes

Materials

Selected Sample Reading Sentences (see Additional Materials at the end of this level)

Selected decodable readers (see Orange Level Chart)

Selected books/stories from your classroom or school library or basal program (suggested book titles appear in Appendix B)

Procedures

In this section we list a variety of options for reading material. The choices you make will depend on the skill level of the students in your group.

Sample Reading Sentences

One of the options in the Orange Level is to provide additional oral reading practice by including pages of Sample Reading Sentences. These can be found in the Additional Materials section at the end of this level.

We have included these sentences because we have found that some decodable readers do not include digraphs and blends until a much later stage (e.g., after students have learned final "e" and vowel teams). The Sample Reading Sentences we have included in the Orange Level provide additional practice reading closed syllable words with digraphs and blends without including more advanced syllable patterns.

Specifically, in the Additional Materials section at the end of this level, the first four pages of Sample Reading Sentences reinforce initial blends, followed by a page that includes final double consonants and initial blends. Next there is a page of Sample Reading Sentences to reinforce final blends and, finally, a page to reinforce blends, final double consonants, and -s endings.

These Sample Reading Sentences reinforce the skills taught thus far in this program.

It is important to note that some of the Sample Reading Sentences may be very challenging for students who still need practice reading words with single consonants and short vowels.

Feel free to shorten the Sample Reading Sentences, select different sentences for different students based on their skills, and substitute words with simpler constructions for any of the words we have included.

It may not be appropriate for all students to read the sentences directly from the lists in the Additional Materials section. Alternative suggestions for presenting these sentences include the following:

- Photocopy the lists on card stock (and enlarge, if necessary).

- Photocopy the lists, cut out the individual sentences, and put the sentences in a box or in a pile on the table.

- Have the students select one or more sentences to read orally.

- Write individual sentences on sentence strips for the students to read.

- Put selected sentences on chart paper, a dry erase board, or the blackboard.

In all cases, if the students make a mistake when reading orally, provide corrective feedback.

Reading Familiar Text

We also encourage you to reread familiar books with all of your students to develop oral reading fluency. As noted in the *Report of the National Reading Panel* (National Institute of Child Health and Human Development, 2000), "Fluent readers are able to read orally with speed, accuracy, and proper expression. Fluency is one of several critical factors for reading comprehension" (p. 11).

We have found that students working at the Orange Level often need additional practice building fluency by reading texts that reinforce simple closed syllable words with single consonants and digraphs as well as closed syllables with blends. The Orange Level decodable book chart provides some examples of books that can be used to provide this practice.

Decodable Book Chart for the Orange Level

To help you select books for your groups, we have created decodable book charts for each of the first five levels of this program. Ideally, each student and teacher should have his or her own copy of each book being read.

> This chart is meant to help you individualize instruction for your students. ***Remember, other decodable books may always be substituted for those on the chart.***
>
>

Although these books are highly decodable (phonetically regular), each book also introduces a small number of high frequency words not previously introduced in this program; these words are also included on the chart.

Orange Level Decodable Book Chart

SV = Steck-Vaughn
MPP = More Primary Phonics
BB B = Bob Books Level B

Step
4

		Decodable Books with Short Vowel Review			
		Title	**Vowels**	**New Words***	**Ending**
1	MPP M1-1	*The Cab*	a		
2	MPP M1-2	*Kim and Wag*	a, i		
3	MPP M1-3	*The Van and the Hot Rod*	a, i, o		
4	MPP M1-4	*Fun in the Mud*	a, i, o, u	*its*	
5	MPP M1-5	*Hal and Nip*	a, i, o, u, e		
6	MPP M1-6	*Cop Cat*	a, i, o, u, e	*too, see*	
7	MPP M1-7	*The Wet Pup*	a, i, o, u, e		
8	MPP M1-8	*The Cod and the Fat Cat*	a, i, o, u, e	*from*	
9	MPP M1-9	*Del*	a, i, o, u, e		
10	MPP M1-10	*Gum on a Cat*	a, i, o, u, e		
		Decodable Books with Double Final Consonants and Blends			
		Title		**New Words***	**Ending**
11	SV 1-10	*Jen's Pet*	Double final consonants	*puts*	
		Decodable Books with Blends			
		Title	**Blends**	**New Words***	**Ending**
12	BB B2-1	*Ten Men*	fl, dr, -nt, -nd, st		
13	BB B2-2	*Bump*	sk, sl, fl, -mp	*over, Sunny, Jimmy, Thumper, Skipper*	*-ed*
14	BB B2-3	*Cat and Mouse*	sk, sn, sl, st, fl, st, -nt	*mouse, Tilly, kitty, house, by, out, too, happy, be*	
15	BB B2-4	*The Swimmers*	st, sw, sl, sp, tr, -nt, -nd, -mp, -lp	*summer, into, want, out, warm, three, swimmers, sunny, happily*	*-ed*

*The *New Words* category in the decodable book chart includes both high frequency words that have not been taught yet in this program and phonetically regular words with patterns that have not been taught yet.

An Important Note About Building Fluency

As previously noted, to build fluency, it is necessary to include **frequent repeated readings** of text and to provide corrective feedback to the students. Students may need to read some of the beginning readers several times to begin to increase fluency.

Additional opportunities for repeated reading can occur by putting completed books in a center where students can reread them at other times during the day. This should not, however, replace repeated reading with corrective feedback by the teacher because repeated reading with corrective feedback has been found to be the most effective method for developing fluency.

An Important Note About Selecting Books

In addition to reading decodable books, students at this level should also have opportunities for supported reading using popular trade books (e.g., easy reading children's books).

At first, you may be doing most of the reading. As students become more proficient, they will be reading more of the text.

Appendix B contains some titles of trade books that students, with support, can successfully read. ***Again, feel free to substitute your favorite books for students reading at this beginning level.***

Step 5 Dictation

5–7 minutes

Materials

Dictation notebook for each student

Pencil

One dry erase board, one dry erase marker, and one eraser for the teacher

Procedures

- Each dictation exercise should include four or five words and one short sentence (four to five words) that uses words with the same phonetic pattern.

- Demonstrate on your dry erase board how students should set up their notebook pages.

- At the beginning of each notebook dictation session, ask the students to put the date on the top of that day's page. This provides an informal method of monitoring each student's day-to-day progress.

- Tell the students which vowels they will be using for that day's lesson. These vowels will be their column headings.

- Have the students write the vowel headings on their page to help organize the dictation.

> Once the students have set up the paper for that day's dictation, review the sounds of the vowels in the vowel headings before dictating the first word.

- Have the students write each word under the appropriate vowel as the word is dictated.

- The sound pack vowel cards from Step 1 corresponding to the vowels that you are using in dictation can be placed on the table as a reference for the students.

Once the students can successfully make words with double final consonants and initial and ending blends on the sound board, you can begin to use these words in dictation. Several examples are provided on the next page.

Examples of notebook dictation pages:

o	*u*	*e*
stop	trunk	wet
hot		left

I was last to run.

a	*e*	*u*
clam	sped	fluff
track	tent	

I can jump and hop.

a	*i*	*o*	*u*
trap	lid	chop	glum
	slid		

Fred is in the club.

a	*i*	*e*
glass	cliff	well
	still	mess

Did Bob miss class?

- Check each student's work and help him or her correct errors (e.g., if a student writes *tap* instead of *trap*, say "You wrote **tap**. I wanted you to write **trrrrrrrrrrrap**. Show me how you would change **tap** to **trap**.")

- When you are pronouncing the words, remember to stretch out the sounds.

- If the student continues to have difficulty, demonstrate for the student on *your* dry erase board, have the student copy the word correctly, and move on to the next word.

- When you dictate the next word, tell the students to say the word slowly and listen for all of the sounds

- After you dictate the individual words, dictate one short sentence (as shown in the sample dication pages).

- Tell the students to write the sentence on a separate line.

- If needed, help the students spell any words in the sentence that can't be sounded out (e.g., *the*).

- At the end of the dictation lesson, have the students read orally all of the words they have written under the vowel headings and also read the sentence.

Step

5

Refer to the Additional Materials section at the end of this level for more sample dictation exercises and additional phonetically regular words that can be used for dictation.

Additional Materials

Orange Level

Phonetically Regular Word Lists (-*ll*, -*ss*, and -*ff*)

-*ll*	-*ss*	-*ff*
Bill	mass	cuff
hill	pass	huff
fill	bass	puff
mill	hiss	Jeff
will	kiss	
chill	miss	
dull	fuss	
hull	Bess	
gull	less	
bell	mess	
fell	Tess	
sell		
tell		
well		
yell		

Orange Level

Phonetically Regular Word Lists (*bl, cl, fl,* and *gl*)

bl	*cl*	*fl*	*gl*
black	clam	flag	glad
bled	clan	flat	glass
bless	clap	flash	glen
bliss	clash	flesh	glob
blob	clip	flex	glum
blot	cliff	flick	
block	click	flop	
blush	clog	flock	
	clock	fluff	
	club	flush	
	cluck		

Orange Level

Phonetically Regular Word Lists (*sk, sl,* and *pl*)

sk
skid
skim
skin
skip
skit
skill
skull

sl	
slab	slit
slam	slick
slap	slob
slack	slop
slash	slot
sled	slush
slid	slug
slim	slip

pl
plum
plop
plan
plug
plot

Orange Level

Phonetically Regular Word Lists

(cr, dr, gr, br, fr, pr, and tr)

cr	dr	gr	br
crab	drag	grab	Brad
crack	dress	grass	brag
crash	drip	grim	brat
crib	drill	grin	brass
crop	drop	grip	brush
crush	drum	grill	

fr	pr	tr	
fret	press	trap	trip
fresh	prop	track	trot
frog	prod	trash	truck
Fran	prom	trim	

Orange Level

Phonetically Regular Word Lists

(*sm, sn, sp, st, sw,* and *tw*)

sm	*sn*	*sp*	*st*	
smack	snag	spam	stab	stop
smash	snap	spat	stash	stub
smell	snack	sped	stack	stun
smug	sniff	spell	staff	stick
	snob	speck	stem	stock
	snuck	spin	step	stuck
	snug	spit	still	stuff
		spill		
		spot		
		spun		

sw	*tw*
swell	twin
swig	twig
swim	
swish	

Orange Level

Phonetically Regular Word Lists (-*mp*, -*sk*, and -*st*)

-*mp*	-*sk*	-*st*
camp	ask	cast
damp	mask	fast
ramp	task	mast
champ	desk	past
limp	risk	nest
romp	dusk	pest
bump	tusk	rest
dump	brisk	fist
jump		list
lump		mist
pump		dust
clump		just
slump		must
thump		rust
plump		twist

Orange Level

Phonetically Regular Word Lists (-*ft*, -*lt*, and -*nt*)

-*ft*	-*lt*	-*nt*
raft	belt	ant
shaft	felt	pant
theft	melt	dent
gift	tilt	sent
lift	wilt	tent
sift	welt	vent
shift		went
		spent
		hint
		lint
		mint
		print
		hunt
		grunt

Orange Level

Phonetically Regular Word Lists (-*lf*, -*lp*, -*nd*, and -*nk*)

-*lf*	-*lp*	-*nd*		-*nk*	
elf	help	and	lend	ink	bunk
self	yelp	band	mend	link	dunk
shelf	gulp	hand	send	mink	junk
	pulp	land	tend	kink	sunk
		gland	spend	pink	chunk
		brand	bond	rink	flunk
		grand	fond	sink	plunk
		stand	pond	think	shrunk
		strand	fund	shrink	
		end			
		bend			

Orange Level

Sample Sound Board Exercises

bl, cl, fl, and gl

1. lock – clock – click – lick – lack – black – block
2. flap – clap – clip – flip – lip – sip – dip
3. black – back – bash – lash – clash – clam – clap
4. black – block – clock – lock – dock – deck – den
5. black – lack – lick – click – cliff – clip – clap
6. flush – blush – bluff – buff – huff – hum – gum

sk, sl, and sp

1. bled – sled – sped – speck – peck – pen – pan
2. lock – clock – click – slick – slim – slit
3. slip – slim – skim – skip – sip – sap – slap
4. slip – slid – sled – sped – spell – sell – sill
5. kit – skit – skin – spin – spill – skill – skid
6. skid – skip – slip – slap – clap – clip – lip

Orange Level

Sample Sound Board Exercises

cr, dr, and gr

1. rip – drip – grip – grid – rid – lid – slid
2. grim – rim – rip – grip – drip – drop – crop
3. rug – rub – grub – grab – crab – cab – lab – slab
4. grill – drill – drip – rip – rib – crib – crab
5. grim – rim – ram – cram – clam – slam – slim
6. bib – rib – crib – crab – grab – grub – rub

Orange Level

Sample Sound Board Exercises*

br, fr, pr, and tr

1. trim – trip – trap – tap – *top* – *drop* – prop

2. rip – grip – trip – trick – *brick* – *thick* – *lick*

3. prom – prim – trim – trip – drip – drill – grill

4. slot – slat – *slap* – *trap* – track – trick – brick

5. trash – rash – rush – *brush* – *mush* – *mesh* – *fresh*

*Starting with the *br, fr, pr,* and *tr* list, students are sometimes asked to make two sound changes (e.g., changing t op to d r op). This may be more challenging for some students. You may need to provide more guidance and point out that two letter cards will be changing. Word pairs that require two sound changes are italicized.

Orange Level

Sample Sound Board Exercises*

sm, sn, sp, st, sw, and tw

1. mug – smug – snug – snag – *snack – back*

2. spell – spill – pill – pin – spin – spit – spot

3. stub – stab – stack – snack – smack – smock – stock

4. tack – stack – snack – snuck – *stuck – truck* – tuck

5. wag – swag – swig – swim – swish – wish – wick

6. sell – smell – spell – swell – swill – still – stick

7. mug – smug – snug – snag – *snack – tack – smack*

8. win – twin – tin – pin – *spin – grin* – grip

*Word pairs that are italicized require two sound changes.

Orange Level

Sample Sound Board Exercises*

-mp, -sk, -st, -ft, -lt, and -nt

1. lift – list – lint – tint – tent – test – best
2. sill – *sell* – *sent* – set – let – left – theft
3. vent – vest – best – bet – belt – felt – fell
4. will – well – welt – melt – met – mat – mast
5. damp – *camp* – *cast* – mast – *mist* – *twist*
6. cat – *cast* – *cap* – camp – *ramp* – *rash* – rush
7. fist – fast – last – list – mist – mast – mask
8. mask – ask – *task* – *tack* – track – *rack* – *ramp*
9. west – went – tent – tint – mint – mist – fist
10. damp – lamp – lump – *jump* – *stump* – *stamp* – *camp*
11. sent – *spent* – *dent* – *desk* – dusk – dust – must
12. *dump* – *dusk* – *husk* – *hump* – lump – limp - lamp

*Word pairs that are italicized require two sound changes.

Orange Level

Sample Sound Board Exercises*

-lf, -lp, -nd, and -nk

1. shell – *sell* – *send* – bend – band – *brand* – *stand*

2. and – land – lend – blend – *blond* – *fond* – pond

3. sunk – *spunk* – *clunk* – *clink* – *clip* – sip – sink

4. *junk* – *jump* – *just* – must – mist – fist – fit

5. link – think – *thin* – *spin* – pin – *pen* – *spend*

6. task – mask – *bask* – *band* – sand – stand – strand

7. *think* – *shrink* – *pink* – *sink* – *blink* – link – ink

8. elf – self – shelf – shell – sell – sill – hill

9. ink – link – mink – wink – *wind* – *wilt* – will

10. hut – hunt – hunk – husk – tusk – task - mask

*Word pairs that are italicized require two sound changes.

Orange Level

Sample Reading Sentences

bl, cl, fl, and gl

1. Bill will get that clam.

2. Jim can miss the class.

3. Beth was glad that Chuck had a pet.

4. Mom did not yell when the glass fell.

5. Flick that tick off his neck!

6. She has her black dog in the pen.

7. Glen did not wish to fall.

8. The black duck will quack.

9. This hen will cluck.

10. Ben will be glad to sell the fish.

11. That clam has a glob in it.

Orange Level

Sample Reading Sentences

sk, sl, and pl

1. You can slip in the slush.

2. Tim did slip in the mud.

3. Beth had a plum.

4. We will all skip and clap.

5. I will lick the plum.

6. I plan to skip the math class.

7. Do you have the skill to sled?

8. The man had a bag of slugs.

9. Jack can skid if the path is slick.

10. Did the fox slip into his den?

Orange Level

Sample Reading Sentences

cr, dr, gr, br, fr, pr, and tr

1. Did Beth grab the frog?

2. The truck fell from the cliff.

3. Did you get that dress?

4. Brad got a drill at the shop.

5. Do not press on the glass!

6. Get the trash from the truck.

7. That is a crack in the crib.

8. Is the fish fresh?

9. He did not brush the dog.

10. Fred got the drum for his dad.

11. Brad did a good trick on the track.

12. Get the truck off the track!

13. I am glad he got the truck.

Orange Level

Sample Reading Sentences

sm, sn, sp, st, sw, and tw

1. Glen slid on the twig.

2. Skip the small stack of stuff.

3. I can smell the snack.

4. Snuff will come when I snap.

5. Fred snuck up on Fran.

6. Do not spill the pills.

7. We will all clap for Dr. Spock.

8. The gum will stick and get stiff.

9. I will mix a speck of this and a spot of that.

10. Liz can snip the tags from the black dress.

11. I wish to swim.

12. The trip will hit a snag.

13. Ben is a twin.

Orange Level

Sample Reading Sentences

-ll, -ss, and -ff

1. Tess will not mess the dress.

2. I can spell well in class.

3. Bill will sell his brass drill.

4. The stuff fell on the grass.

5. The dress is still on the doll.

6. The swell bell fell on the grass.

7. Mom will yell if I spill my glass.

8. We will pass the class and do well.

9. Press the cuff on the dress.

10. We will have less mess if we fill the glass.

Orange Level

Sample Reading Sentences

-mp, -sk, -st, -ft, -lt, and -nt

1. I felt damp when I was at the dump.

2. It was a risk to get up to the nest.

3. The slush will melt fast.

4. I will ask Mom to get the gift.

5. I went to the camp with the mask.

6. The champ has a cast on his leg.

7. She fell from the bed with a thump.

8. Fred did not punt the ball.

9. Get the raft fast!

10. The limp is from the cut.

11. The duck had fluff on his back.

12. She left the class.

Orange Level

Sample Reading Sentences

blends and -s endings

1. The lad picks up the trash.

2. Ted skips up the steps.

3. The cat jumps on the bug.

4. The crab digs in mud.

5. A big shell sits on the sand.

6. I had snacks with my lunch.

7. The glass will crack if it drops.

8. The tint helps block the sun.

9. The kid hops and skips for fun.

10. Jeff jumps and swims in the pond.

11. My dog has lots of spots on his legs.

12. The tot spills a lot of his drinks.

13. I got crabs and frogs from the pond.

14. The kid picks up his blocks.

15. Mom smells fresh when she hugs me.

Orange Level

Sample Dictation Exercises

bl, cl, fl, and gl

<u>**e**</u>
bled
bless

<u>**a**</u>
clam
lap

The clam stuck to the pot.

<u>**u**</u>
fluff
flush

<u>**a**</u>
glad
lad

Ben is glad to sell the fish.

sk, sl, sp, and pl

<u>**i**</u>
skip
lip

<u>**e**</u>
sled

<u>**a**</u>
plan

We will skip to class.

Orange Level

Sample Dictation Exercises

cr, gr, br, fr, and tr

<u>**a**</u>
map
grab

<u>**i**</u>
trim
grip

Get a grip on that crab.

<u>**a**</u>
brat
rag

<u>**e**</u>
fresh
fret

Brad got a fish.

Orange Level

Sample Dictation Exercises

sm, sn, sp, st, sw, and tw

a	**o**
mash	spot
snack	snob

We will swim.

i	**e**	**o**
swim	wet	stop
twig		

The twig is in the mud.

-mp, -sk, -st, -ft, -lt, and -nt

a	**u**
damp	dump
mask	hut
last	

It is damp at the dump.

a	**e**
ran	left
ant	felt

The last tent is up.

Orange Level

Sample Dictation Exercises

-lf, -lp, -nd, and -nk

<u>**a**</u>
and
pan

<u>**e**</u>
elf
help

Help Sam get on the bunk.

<u>**i**</u>
lift

<u>**u**</u>
fun

<u>**e**</u>
lend
bend

He will lend a hand.

-Yellow Level-

Skills to Review

 1 Identify all consonant sounds.

 2 Identify the five short vowel sounds.

 3 Identify the digraphs *th, ch, sh,* and *-ck.*

 4 Read and spell closed syllable words with all five short vowels and single consonants (e.g., *sip*).

 5 Read and spell closed syllable words with the digraphs *th, ch, sh,* and *-ck* (e.g., *lock*).

 6 Read and spell closed syllable words with double final consonants *-ll, -ss,* and *-ff* (e.g., *well, miss, puff*).

 7 Read and spell closed syllable words with initial blends (e.g., *slip*).

 8 Read and spell closed syllable words with final blends (e.g., *fast*).

 9 Read and spell closed syllable words with *-s* and *-ing* when there is no change to the spelling of the base word (e.g., *hats, jumps, rocking, fishing*).

Goals for the Yellow Level

When the students complete this level, they should be able to do the following:

⭐1 Read and spell final "e" words with *a-e* (e.g., **ap<u>e</u>**), *i-e* (e.g., k<u>ite</u>), *o-e* (e.g., **b<u>one</u>**), *u-e* (e.g., **m<u>ule</u>, <u>use</u>**), and *e-e* (e.g., **<u>eve</u>**) with single consonants.

⭐2 Read and spell final "e" words with consonant digraphs (e.g, **<u>sh</u>ade**) and consonant blends (e.g., **<u>fl</u>ame, <u>st</u>ove**).

⭐3 Read open, one-syllable words (e.g., *he, so, me, go*), including words ending in *y* (e.g, *cr<u>y</u>, fl<u>y</u>*).

⭐4 Read words with *-ed* and recognize that *-ed* can have three sounds: the *-ed* in *rest<u>ed</u>*, the *-ed* that sounds like the /d/ in *fill<u>ed</u>*, and the *-ed* that sounds like the /t/ in *wish<u>ed</u>*.

⭐5 Read compound words made up of previously learned syllable patterns (e.g., *sunset, fishnet, cupcake, jumprope, backpack*) and two-syllable words with two consonants between two vowels (e.g., *rabbit, napkin*) creating two closed syllables.

Please note: Although we have identified reading two-syllable words as one of the **Yellow Level** goals, it may not be appropriate for all students at this time.

Students who can read closed, final "e," and open syllables fluently are ready to combine these syllables into two-syllable words. For these students, it is appropriate to introduce simple rules for syllable division, such as how you would divide *rabbit* and *napkin*.

For students who are not yet automatic at the one-syllable word level, it may be appropriate to wait until you get to the **Green Level**, when one-syllable words are more automatic, to introduce multisyllabic words.

Step 1

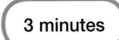

(3 minutes)

Review Sound–Symbol Correspondences

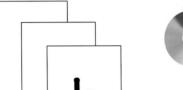

Step 1

Materials

CD Sound pack cards (sounds for review and new sounds)

Procedures

Use your sound pack of previously learned letters to quickly review the letter names and sounds with your students. Remember, the goal is to develop fluency, not boredom.

> You probably will not need to continue to review all of the consonants at this point. You should, however, continue to review any consonants (e.g., *b, d, x, y, w*) that the students do not know automatically, as well as the consonant digraphs *th, ch, sh, wh, ph* (*wh* and *ph* are added as new digraphs at this level), and *-ck* and the five short vowels.

Final "e"

As the students learn the final "e" syllable type, the vowel graphemes (e.g., *a-e* as in *c**ak**e*) should be added to the sound pack.

Put two dots in the upper right corner on the *u-e* sound card, as the students will be learning two sounds for this grapheme: *u-e* as in ***use*** and *u-e* as in *t**un**e*.

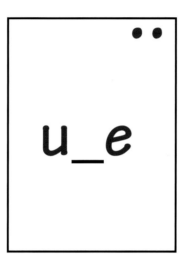

Y as a Vowel

Introduce *y* as a vowel by teaching the students the sound of /y/ at the end of open, one-syllable words (e.g., *sl**y**, cr**y**, m**y**, fl**y***).

This *y* will be color-coded red to indicate that it is functioning as a vowel.

Step 2

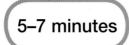

Teach or Review New Decoding Skill

5–7 minutes

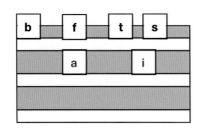

 Step 2

Materials

 CD Sound board for each student

 CD Consonant letters and digraphs in the top pocket (only include those needed to make words for a particular lesson)

 CD Vowel letters in the middle pocket (only include those needed to make words for a particular lesson)

One dry erase board, one dry erase marker, and one eraser for the teacher

Procedures

Once the students can make words with short vowels on the sound board, use the sound board to introduce final "e" words with single consonants and final "e" words with consonant blends. Later, open, one-syllable words will be introduced.

Final "e"

Use the sound board to demonstrate what happens to a closed syllable (short vowel) word when you add the final "e."

138

Start by using the *a-e* list below, and have students make **six to eight** closed syllable words with short /a/ into final "e" words. For example, first have the students make **can** on the sound board using the procedure introduced in previous lessons. Next, show the students what happens when you add a final "e" to **can**.

Step
2

_a-e_		**_i-e_**		**_o-e_**	
can	------► cane	pin	------► pine	not	------► note
cap	------► cape	hid	------► hide	rob	------► robe
van	------► vane	rid	------► ride	rod	------► rode
man	------► mane	bit	------► bite	hop	------► hope
rat	------► rate	dim	------► dime	cop	------► cope
mad	------► made	Tim	------► time	mop	------► mope
at	------► ate	kit	------► kite		
Sam	------► same	rip	------► ripe		
mat	------► mate	fin	------► fine		
tap	------► tape				

_u-e_		**_e-e_**	
cub	------► cube	pet	------► Pete
tub	------► tube		
cut	------► cute		

After practicing the pairs to introduce each final "e" pattern, reinforce each pattern in the follow-up lessons by using a more traditional sound board sequence such as the following (read across):

cap ------→ cape ------→ tape ------→ tap ------→ map ------→ mat ------→ mate

For sample sound board exercises with the final "e" pattern and single consonants, see the Additional Materials section at the end of this level.

Once the students can make words with final "e" with single consonants on the sound board, use the sound board to demonstrate what happens when you add blends and digraphs to final "e" words.

For example, have students make the following words:

_a-e_	_i-e_	_o-e_
lane ------→ plane	pike ------→ spike	tone ------→ stone
ate ------→ skate	mile ------→ smile	lope* ------→ slope
late ------→ slate	pine ------→ spine	rove ------→ grove
late ------→ plate	wipe ------→ swipe	cone ------→ clone*
take ------→ stake	ride ------→ bride	
rave ------→ brave	ripe ------→ gripe	
ape ------→ grape		
ale ------→ stale		
fake ------→ flake		

*Do your students know the meaning of the words **lope** and **clone**?

If not, this is a good opportunity to expand vocabulary.

Next, demonstrate what happens when you add a final "e" to a closed syllable word with a blend. For example, students can make the following words:

	a-e			*i-e*	
glad	----->	glade	spin	----->	spine
slat	----->	slate	twin	----->	twine
grad	----->	grade	slim	----->	slime
plan	----->	plane	slid	----->	slide

Once the students can make the **pairs** with the blends, you can go back to making **lists** and changing only one sound, or occasionally two sounds (e.g., **gr**ime, **d**ime), at a time.

For example (read across)

rim -----> grim -----> grime -----> dime -----> lime -----> slime -----> chime

See the Additional Materials section at the end of this level for more examples of sound board exercises.

Open, One-Syllable Words

Students will be encountering two- and three-letter words that end in a vowel (e.g., g**o**, sh**e**) in the books they are reading. These are considered open syllables. They end in a single vowel, and the vowel has the long sound.

Although many of these words have already been learned as sight words (e.g., *we, he*), it is helpful to introduce these words on the dry erase board (and later on the sound board) to help students see the pattern.

Using your dry erase board, list the following words:

- Review with the students that when a vowel is at the end of a two- or three-letter word, it says the long sound (i.e., it says its name).

- Demonstrate this by reading the first few words on the list and asking the students to read the rest of the words.

- Next, show the students what happens when you add a consonant to the end of the word (i.e., when you "close up" the vowel), as illustrated on the next page.

For example, show the students how you can make

me	------>	met
he	------>	hen
we	------>	wet
be	------>	bed
she	------>	shed
so	------>	sob
no	------>	not
go	------>	got
hi	------>	hit

Once you have practiced these words on the dry erase board, include them in more traditional sound board lessons, as shown in the example below:

bled ------> bed ------> be ------> bet ------> bent ------> went ------> we

Another group of open syllable words includes two- and three-letter words that end in *y* (e.g., *by, fly, spy*). In these words, *y* is acting as a vowel, and it makes the sound of long /i/.

- First, review the words listed below on the dry erase board. Explain to the students that *y* is acting as a vowel and makes the sound of long /i/.

by

my

cry

dry

fry

sky

- Next, use the red *y* card for the sound board and practice making simple open syllable words that end in *y* on the sound board.

Sound board lists might look like the following:

shy ----→ dry ----→ cry ----→ my ----→ try ----→ why ----→ fly

by ----→ why ----→ my ----→ sty ----→ spry* ----→ cry ----→ fry

See the Additional Materials section at the end of this level for lists of open, one-syllable words.

*Do your students know what **spry** means?

Step
2

Step 3

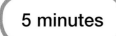

5 minutes

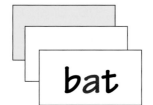

bat

Review Phonetically Regular Words (PRWs) and High Frequency Words (HFWs)

Materials

Phonetically regular word (PRW) cards (only those words you plan to use in a particular lesson)

High frequency word (HFW) cards (only those words that you plan to use in a particular lesson)

One dry erase board, one dry erase marker, and one eraser for the teacher

Procedures

The goal of this activity is to develop fluency. The focus is on the phonetically regular words, with a few high frequency words included. Each student in a group should have about three turns to read words. If you have a group of five students, for example, you might start off with about 15–20 words. At first, 10–15 words would be phonetically regular words and 5 would be high frequency words.

Phonetically Regular Words (PRWs)

As in previous levels, the phonetically regular words and high frequency words should not be written on the same color cards.

The phonetically regular words would consist of words with the new patterns you are teaching (final "e" with single consonants, digraphs, and consonant blends; open syllables [e.g., *he, cry*]; and compound words).

Step

3

Words with previously learned syllable patterns (e.g., closed syllables with single consonants, digraphs and blends) should also be included in your phonetically regular word cards and reviewed.

Words with the new digraph *wh* (**wh**ip, **wh**iff, **wh**en, **wh**iplash) and the new digraph *ph* (**ph**one) also should be included.

> This step includes starter sets of phonetically regular words arranged by the patterns you are teaching. As shown in the starter set, make sure to write the consonants in black and the vowels in red.

Final "e" Words with Single Consonants

- Once the students can successfully make final "e" words with *a-e* and single consonants (e.g., c*ake*) on the sound board, you can add words with *a-e* to your phonetically regular word (PRW) cards and introduce words with *i-e* on the sound board.

- Follow the same procedure with words with *i-e* (e.g., k*ite*), *o-e* (e.g., b*one*), *u-e* (e.g., m*ule*, *use*), and *e-e* (e.g., *eve*), adding words with those patterns to the phonetically regular word (PRW) cards as soon as students can make those words on the sound board.

Step 3

Starter Set of Yellow Level Phonetically Regular Word (PRW) Cards

Final "e" with single consonants

a-e	i-e	o-e	u-e	e-e
date	ride	hole	mule	Pete
rake	ripe	mole	cube	eve
take	bite	rope	cute	
tape	bike	bone	fuse	
safe	time	hope	rude	
rate	side	vote	rule	
wade	hide	joke	tube	
fade	line	pole	tune	
late	dime	robe	dune	
same	pipe	cone	mute	

Final "e" Words with Blends and Digraphs

- When the students can successfully make final "e" words with *a-e* and blends (e.g., *flake*) on the sound board, you can add words with *a-e* and blends to your phonetically regular word (PRW) cards and introduce words with *i-e* and blends (e.g., *slide*) on the sound board.

- Follow the same procedure with words with *i-e* (e.g., *slide*), *o-e* (e.g., *stone*), *u-e* (e.g., *flute*), and *e-e* (e.g., *Steve*), adding words with these patterns to the phonetically regular word (PRW) cards as soon as students can make those words on the sound board.

Step 3

Starter Set of Yellow Level Phonetically Regular Word (PRW) Cards

Final "e" with blends and digraphs

a-e	*i-e*	*o-e*	*u-e*	*e-e*
shade	slide	choke	flute	Steve
flame	chime	slope		

The Additional Materials section at the end of this level contains additional lists of final "e" words with single consonants, digraphs, and blends.

Open, One-Syllable Words

It is also a good idea to reinforce two- and three-letter words that end in a vowel (e.g., *go, she*) in this step of the lesson. As mentioned in Step 2, these words are considered open syllables. They end in a single vowel, and the vowel has the long sound. Although many of these words have already been learned as sight words (e.g., *we, he*), students should now be able to see the pattern.

The other group of open syllable words taught in Step 2 includes two- and three-letter words that end in *y* (e.g., *by, my, fly, cry, dry, fry, spy, sky*). Remind the students that in these words the *y* is acting as a vowel and makes the sound of long /i/.

Gradually add these words to your phonetically regular word (PRW) cards, remembering to write the *y* in red.

Starter Set of Yellow Level Phonetically Regular Word (PRW) Cards

Open syllables

o	*e*	*y*
go	he	cry
so	me	fly
	we	

See the Additional Materials section at the end of this level for lists of open, one-syllable words.

Words with the Inflected Ending -ed (Minilesson)

It is helpful to introduce the -ed concept in this step of the lesson.

Use your dry erase board to introduce the concept by writing the following three sentences, one at a time:

- I **_lifted_** the box. (The -ed makes the expected /ed/ sound.)

- I **_spilled_** the can. (The -ed makes the /d/ sound.)

- I **_picked_** up the cat. (The -ed makes the /t/ sound.)

Underline the -ed in each sentence. Point out that in each sentence, something has happened in the past. One way we know that something has already happened is because there is an -ed added to the action word (verb).

This is also the time to explain to the students that -ed makes three different sounds: /ed/ as in lift**_ed_**, /d/ as in spill**_ed_**, and /t/ as in pick**_ed_**. Reread each sentence, and listen for the three different sounds.

Add words with -ed that do not require a change to the base word (e.g., rest + ed = rested) to your phonetically regular word (PRW) cards.

For example, select words from the following:

/ed/	**/d/**	**/t/**
rested	filled	wished
lifted	smelled	picked

- Put -ed on a separate card from the base word. First, ask a student to read the word card with the base word (e.g., *rest*).

rest

Step
3

- Then, put the -ed card next to the card with the base word on it, and ask a student to read the new word (e.g., *rested*).

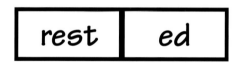

Refer to the Additional Materials section at the end of this level for lists of words with the inflected -ed ending with no change to the base word.

Compound Words

In this level, you will also be introducing compound words made up of the syllable types the students have already learned (i.e., closed and final "e").

Compound words, such as *sunset, cupcake, whiplash,* and *backpack,* can be put on white index cards for review, as you would with any other phonetically regular words in this step.

- For some groups, you might want to review the one-syllable words first, and then (when you get to the compound word cards) say, "Now, we are going to try some harder words."

- The first time you introduce compound words, it may be helpful to introduce the individual words (e.g., *back, pack*) on separate cards.

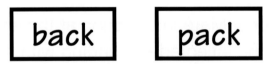

- Next, physically move the cards together to show the students how compound words are made up of words they already know how to read.

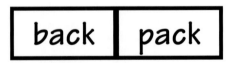

The number of compound words you include at this step will depend on the group's automaticity with one-syllable words.

Groups Moving Quickly

Groups moving quickly can read many compound words in this step.

Groups Needing More Practice

To introduce compound words to groups needing more practice, it is helpful to first introduce compound words made up of two closed syllables with single consonants (e.g., *sunset*).

- Put *sun* and *set* on individual cards, and have the students read the individual words.

- Next, move the cards together, and have the students read the compound word.

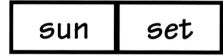

- If the students are successful reading a compound word, include the word in the phonetically regular word (PRW) cards the following day.

Once the students can read compound words using only closed syllables, introduce words using closed syllables and final "e" syllables (e.g., *pancake*).

> If students find these words difficult at this level, continue to focus on one-syllable words and reintroduce compound words at the next level.

Two-Syllable Words (such as *rabbit, napkin*)

For students who were successful reading compound words, the next step is to introduce two-syllable words with two consonants between two vowels (e.g., *rabbit, napkin*). Write the following words on the dry erase board:

Step

3

> **ra<u>bb</u>it**
>
> **mi<u>tt</u>en**
>
> **mu<u>ff</u>in**
>
> **pu<u>pp</u>et**

- Underline the double letters in the middle of the word (e.g., *ra**bb**it*). Tell the students that when they see double letters (consonants) in the middle of a word, they can break the word into two little parts. This will help them read the word.

- Demonstrate by drawing a line between the *b/b* in *rab/bit*. Next to *rab/bit* on the dry erase board, write the two parts (syllables) separated by a space. Draw a line under the two parts to show the students how to "scoop" the two parts and read the whole word.

rab/bit   rab   bit

- Have the students read the two parts and then say the whole word quickly. Follow the same procedure for the next three words (*mitten, muffin,* and *puppet*) on your dry erase board.

On the following day, repeat this procedure using the following words:

> **ki<u>tt</u>en**
>
> **te<u>nn</u>is**
>
> **tra<u>ff</u>ic**
>
> **ma<u>tt</u>ress**

Once the students can read these words on the dry erase board, gradually add them to your phonetically regular word (PRW) cards.

When students can read words like *rabbit,* use the dry erase board to introduce two-syllable words with two *different* consonants between two vowels (e.g., *napkin*).

Write the following words on the dry erase board:

> **na<u>pk</u>in**
>
> **go<u>bl</u>in**
>
> **ba<u>sk</u>et**
>
> **ma<u>gn</u>et**

- Underline the two consonants in the middle of the word (e.g., *na**pk**in*).

- Tell the students that when they see two consonants between two vowels in the middle of a word, they can break the word into two little parts. This will help them read the word.

- Demonstrate by drawing a line between the *p* and the *k* in *nap/kin*. Next to *nap/kin* on the dry erase board, write the two parts (syllables) separated by a space. Draw a line under the two parts to show the students how to "scoop" the two parts and read the whole word.

nap/kin   **nap kin**

Step
3

- Have the students read the two parts and then say the whole word quickly. Follow the same procedure for the next three words (*goblin, basket,* and *magnet*) on the dry erase board.

On the following day, repeat this procedure using the following words:

> **picnic**
>
> **dentist**
>
> **contest**
>
> **splendid**

Once the students can read these words on the dry erase board, gradually add them to your phonetically regular word (PRW) cards.

For some students, you might want to first review the one-syllable words that you have included in your phonetically regular word (PRW) cards in this step. Then, when you get to the two-syllable word cards, say, "Now, we are going to try some of our challenge words."

The number of two-syllable words you include in your PRW cards for review in this step will depend on the students' fluency with one-syllable words.

Refer to the Additional Materials section at the end of this level for a list of compound words and two-syllable words with two consonants between two vowels, such as *napkin*, as well as lists of final "e" words and words with the inflected *-ed* ending that you can include in this step. Add these words to your phonetically regular word (PRW) cards.

High Frequency Words (HFWs) 101–150

The following high frequency words (HFWs) from Fry and Kress (2006) can be taught and added to your word card pack. You might want to pretest the students on these HFWs at this level and create an individualized list of HFWs that the students still need to learn. A High Frequency Word Assessment form for the Yellow Level and individual word cards are included on the CD-ROM.

over	new	sound	**take	only	little	work
know	place	year	live	**me	*back	give
most	very	after	thing	our	*just	**name
good	sentence	*man	think	say	great	where
*help	through	*much	before	**line	right	too
mean	old	any	**same	*tell	boy	follow
**came	want	show	also	around	farm	three
small						

Adapted from *The Reading Teacher's Book of Lists, Fifth Edition,* by E.B. Fry and J. Kress
© 2006 Jossey-Bass. Reprinted with permission from John Wiley & Sons, Inc.

*Students learned to decode words written in red and orange during the Red Level and Orange Level in this program, respectively.

**Students will be learning to decode the words written in yellow at this level in the program. These words are phonetically regular.

Step
3

Once each high frequency word has been learned by most of the students, it is a good idea to file the word in alphabetical order in the back of a high frequency word box. These words should be reviewed on a regular basis in Step 3 of your lesson to make sure that the students remember them.

An Important Note About Developing Fluency

Remember, the overall goal of this activity is to develop fluency at the word level. A hallmark of good readers is the ability to read both accurately and fluently.

To help students develop fluency, you will need to have them read the words more than once. The first time the words are read, the goal is accuracy. If a student misreads a vowel in a word (reading *made* as *mad*), it helps to point to the vowel and the final "e" and ask the student to tell you the sound the vowel makes when there is a final "e." Then, ask the student to read the entire word. If the student continues to read the word incorrectly, then pronounce the word for the student and move on.

Activities for Developing Fluency

- When the students read the words for the second time, try using an hourglass to encourage the students to move more quickly. The students like to see how many words they can read before the sand runs out.

- Use a stopwatch with the group and have the students see how long it takes to read all of the words in the card pack for that day. As you go around the group, you can accommodate a student who reads less fluently by asking that student to read a word that you know he or she can read. This ensures that each student gets a turn and keeps the activity moving.

- Students can also use the hourglass and stopwatch while working in pairs. Each student tries to read his or her words more quickly than during his or her previous reading. This way, the students are encouraged to improve their own times and not compete with each other.

Step 4

Read Orally in Context

10–15 minutes

Materials

Selected decodable readers (see **Yellow Level** Chart)

Selected books/stories from your classroom or school library or basal program (suggested book titles appear in Appendix B)

Procedures

In this section we list a variety of options for reading material. The choices you make will depend on the skill level of your students.

You should start to increase the amount of time you spend on oral reading during each lesson. ***It is also important to make sure that students have opportunities to read orally with corrective feedback at other times during the day.***

Remember that all time guidelines given are only suggestions to help plan each lesson. Times may need to be adjusted (up or down) for each step, depending on the needs of your students.

Step

4

We encourage you to reread familiar books with all of your students to develop oral reading fluency. As noted in the *Report of the National Reading Panel* (National Institute of Child Health and Human Development, 2000), "Fluent readers are able to read orally with speed, accuracy, and proper expression. Fluency is one of several critical factors for reading comprehension" (p. 11).

Decodable Book Chart for the Yellow Level

To help you select books for your groups, we have created decodable book charts for each of the first five levels of this program. Ideally, each student and teacher should have his or her own copy of each book being read.

Books on this chart are arranged by the final "e" patterns being taught in this level.

This chart is meant to help you individualize instruction for your students. **Remember, other decodable books may be substituted for those on the chart.**

Although these books are highly decodable (phonetically regular), each book also introduces a small number of high frequency words not previously introduced in this program; these words are also included on the chart.

Yellow Level Decodable Book Chart

SV = Steck-Vaughn   PP = Primary Phonics
                         MPP = More Primary Phonics

			Title	Vowel Focus	New Words*	Ending
			Decodable Books with Final "e"			
1	PP 2-2		*The Big Game*	*a-e, i-e*	hope, home	
2	SV 2-3		*Five Mice and Mike*	*a-e, i-e*	see	
3	SV 2-4		*The Big Bike*	*a-e, i-e*	tie	
4	PP 2-1		*Mac Gets Well*	*a-e, i-e, o-e*		
5	PP 2-3		*The Joke*	*a-e, i-e, o-e*		
6	MPP M2-4		*A Ride on a Bus*	*a-e, i-e, o-e*		
7	MPP M2-1		*Babe, the Big Hit*	*a-e, i-e, o-e*	cute	-ed
8	MPP M2-2		*Make the Bed*	*a-e, i-e, o-e*	rule, your	
9	MPP M2-3		*Mole*	*a-e, i-e, o-e*		
10	SV 2-5		*Miss Duke's Mule*	*a-e, i-e, u-e*		's
11	SV 2-6		*Sue and Jule*	*a-e, i-e, u-e*	Sue, grandma, suit, puts, wait,	
12	PP 2-4		*The Cake*	*a-e, i-e, o-e, u-e*		

*The *New Words* category in the decodable book chart includes both high frequency words that have not been taught yet in this program and phonetically regular words with patterns that have not been taught yet.

Step
4

An Important Note About Building Fluency

As previously noted, to build fluency, it is necessary to include **frequent repeated readings** of text and to provide corrective feedback to the students. Students may need to read some of the readers several times to increase fluency.

Additional opportunities for repeated reading can occur by putting completed books in a center where students can reread them at other times during the day. This should not, however, replace repeated reading with corrective feedback by the teacher because repeated reading with corrective feedback has been found to be the most effective method for developing fluency.

An Important Note About Selecting Books

In addition to reading decodable books, students at this level should also have opportunities for supported reading using popular trade books.

Although many students may be proficient enough to read most of the text in carefully selected trade books, others may continue to need more support from the teacher (e.g., needing the teacher to supply unknown words or alternating reading when texts become longer, as in chapter books).

Appendix B contains some titles of trade books that students, with support, will be able to read successfully. **Again, feel free to substitute your favorite books for students reading at this level.**

Step 5 Dictation

5–7 minutes

Materials

Dictation notebook for each student

Pencil

One dry erase board, one dry erase marker, and one eraser for the teacher

Procedures

- Each dictation exercise should include five or six words and one short sentence that uses words with the same phonetic pattern.

- At the beginning of each notebook dictation session, ask the students to put the date on the top of that day's page. This provides an informal method of monitoring each student's day-to-day progress.

- Tell the students which vowels they will be using for that day's lesson. These vowels will be their column headings.

- Have the students write the vowel headings on their page to help organize the dictation.

Once the students have set up the paper for that day's dictation, review the sounds of the vowels in the vowel headings before dictating the first word.

- Have the students write each word under the appropriate vowel as the word is dictated.

- The sound pack vowel cards from Step 1 corresponding to the vowels that you are using in dictation can be placed on the table as a reference for the students.

Once students can successfully make words with final "e" (e.g., *a-e* as in c*a*k*e*) on the sound board and you have included that pattern in other steps of the lesson, you can begin to use words with that pattern in dictation.

Likewise, once the students can make words with final "e" and blends and digraphs (e.g., *plate, shine*) on the sound board and you have included that pattern in other steps of the lesson, you can begin to use words with that pattern in dictation.

If your students are ready to write a compound word (e.g., *cupcake*), explain to the students that that word will **not** go under one of the vowel headings. That word can be a challenge word that is written on a separate line (not using the headings) before you dictate the sentence (see example on next page). You can also use a compound word in the sentence if your students are reading these words correctly in Step 3.

In this level, focus the dictation exercises on final "e" syllables with single consonants, digraphs, and blends, paying special attention to contrasting long and short vowels, as shown below.

Examples of notebook dictation pages: Final "e"

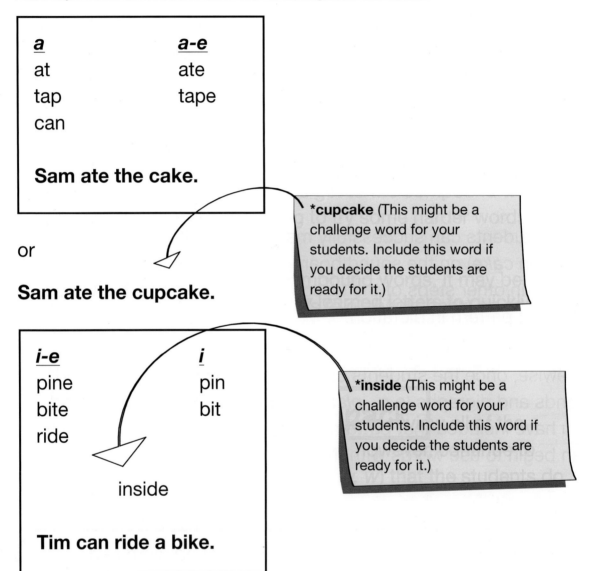

_a_   **_a-e_**
at   ate
tap   tape
can

Sam ate the cake.

or

Sam ate the cupcake.

*cupcake (This might be a challenge word for your students. Include this word if you decide the students are ready for it.)

_i-e_   **_i_**
pine   pin
bite   bit
ride

inside

Tim can ride a bike.

*inside (This might be a challenge word for your students. Include this word if you decide the students are ready for it.)

Step
5

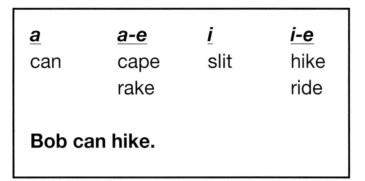

a	*a-e*	*i*	*i-e*
can	cape	slit	hike
	rake		ride

Bob can hike.

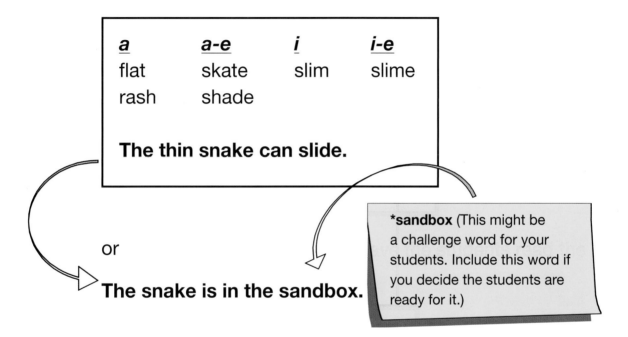

a	*a-e*	*i*	*i-e*
flat	skate	slim	slime
rash	shade		

The thin snake can slide.

or

The snake is in the sandbox.

*sandbox (This might be a challenge word for your students. Include this word if you decide the students are ready for it.)

- Check each student's work and help him or her correct errors.

- If the student continues to have difficulty, demonstrate for the student on *your* dry erase board, have the student copy the word correctly, and move on to the next word.

Refer to the Additional Materials section at the end of this level for more sample dictation exercises.

Step 5

Additional Materials

Yellow Level

Phonetically Regular Word Lists (*a-e* and *i-e*)

a-e		*i-e*	
rake	Dave	pile	file
ate	cape	fine	mile
hate	game	pine	hide
tape	base	dime	rise
wade	made	kite	lime
fake	same	pipe	mine
lake	mane	vine	like
sane	case	bike	life
lame	tame	bite	size
late		time	side
sale		ripe	tile
gaze		nine	hike
bake		tide	
fade		line	
cave		wife	

Phonetically Regular Word Lists (*o-e, u-e,* and *e-e*)

o-e		u-e (mule)	u-e (rule)
hope	yoke	cube	rude
wove	mode	mute	rule
tote	cone	cute	tune
tone	pole	fuse	tube
hone	bone	use	dune
cope	lone		duke
mole	mope		
home	hole		
lobe	zone		
vote	robe		
joke	rope		

e-e
eve
Pete

173

Yellow Level

Phonetically Regular Word Lists

(*a-e* and *i-e* with blends and digraphs)

a-e		i-e	
blade	shake	bride	stride
brave	skate	chime	swipe
crane	slate	crime	tribe
crate	slave	drive	twine
flake	snake	glide	while
flame	stake	pride	whine
frame	stale	prize	white
glade	state	shrine	
grade	trade	slide	
grape	whale	slime	
plane		smile	
plate		spike	
quake		spine	

Phonetically Regular Word Lists

(*o-e, u-e,* and *e-e* with blends and digraphs)

o-e		u-e	e-e
broke	stoke	fluke	Steve
choke	stole	flute	theme
chose	stone		these
clone	stove		
clove	stroke		
drove	those		
froze	throne		
grove			
phone			
quote			
slope			
smoke			

Phonetically Regular Word Lists (open syllables)

e
be
he
me
she
we

o
go
no
so
yo-yo

y	
by	sky
cry	sly
dry	spy
fly	spry
fry	sty
my	try
ply	why
shy	

i
hi

u
flu

Yellow Level

Phonetically Regular Word Lists

(inflected -*ed* ending with no change to base word)

-*ed*	/d/	/t/
rested	filled	wished
lifted	smelled	fixed
landed	thrilled	jumped
hunted	spelled	helped
melted	spilled	picked
twisted		

Yellow Level

Phonetically Regular Word Lists

(compound words with closed syllables)

sunset	dishpan
suntan	bathtub
cobweb	hotshot
cannot	backpack
catnip	whiplash
dishrag	bobsled
uphill	sunlamp
upset	himself
hubcap	landfill
sunlit	catfish
pigpen	sandbox
bedbug	handstand
bobcat	granddad

Yellow Level

Phonetically Regular Word Lists

(compound words with closed and final "e" syllables)

pancake	cupcake
update	inside
sunrise	wishbone
manhole	nickname
pothole	shipmate
tadpole	sidestep
hillside	windpipe
pipeline	whalebone
sunshine	handshake
flagpole	bedside
baseline	backbone
bagpipe	rosebud
classmate	campsite
homesick	

Phonetically Regular Word Lists

(two-syllable words with two consonants between two vowels—VCCV)

absent	magnet	public
basket	mitten	publish
contest	muffins	rabbit
dentist	napkin	splendid
flatten	picnic	sudden
happen	puppets	until
helmet	plastic	
insist	problem	

Yellow Level

Sample Sound Board Exercises

(closed syllable and final "e" pairs with single consonants)

a-e	i-e	o-e
at → ate	rid → ride	mop → mope
mat → mate	rip → ripe	hop → hope
mad → made	bit → bite	cop → cope
fad → fade	fin → fine	cod → code
tap → tape	pin → pine	rod → rode
man → mane	din → dine	rob → robe
Sam → same	Sid → side	not → note
Jan → Jane	hid → hide	
can → cane	Tim → time	
cap → cape	dim → dime	
Sal → sale	kit → kite	
van → vane		
hat → hate		
rat → rate		

Sample Sound Board Exercises

(closed syllable and final "e" pairs with single consonants)

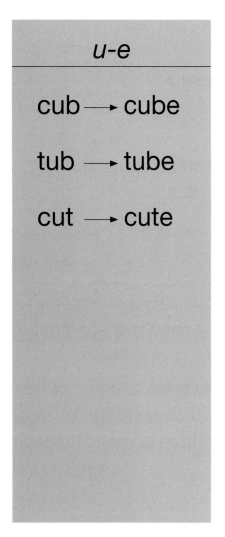

u-e

cub ⟶ cube

tub ⟶ tube

cut ⟶ cute

e-e

pet ⟶ Pete

Yellow Level

Sample Sound Board Exercises

a-e

1. make – take – fake – fame – same – came – cane
2. mad – made – mane – man – pan – pane – lane
3. ape – tape – tap – cap – cape – cake – bake
4. fad – fade – fame – same – Sam – Sal – sale
5. can – cane – vane – van – man – mane – make

i-e

1. ride – hide – tide – tile – mile – pile – pine
2. pin – pine – fine – fin – bin – bit – bite
3. Tim – time – dime – dim – din – dine – mine
4. rid – ride – ripe – rip – sip – Sid – side
5. hide – hid – rid – ride – wide – wipe – pipe

Sample Sound Board Exercises

a-e and i-e

1. bike – bake – take – tame – time – dime – dim
2. tile – tale – male – mile – pile – pale – pal
3. pin – pine – pane – pan – man – mane – mine
4. vine – vane – van – fan – fin – fine – line
5. lake – like – Mike – make – made – fade – fad

o-e

1. rope – hope – home – hole – pole – poke – joke
2. rob – robe – rode – rod – cod – code – cone
3. mop – mope – rope – rote – rot – not – note
4. con – cone – cope – cop – hop – hope – home
5. bone – tone – tote – tot – not – note – nope

Sample Sound Board Exercises

a-e, i-e, and o-e

1. pale – pile – pole – mole – mile – male – sale
2. wade – wide – ride – rode – code – cope – cape
3. not – note – rote – rate – rake – lake – like
4. lane – lone – line – mine – mane – cane – cone
5. rope – ripe – pipe – pine – pane – lane – lone
6. rose – pose – poke – woke – wake – wade – wide

u-e

1. rude – rule – mule – mute – cute – cube – tube
2. cut – cute – cube – cub – tub – tube – tune
3. tune – dune – duke – dude – dud

Sample Sound Board Exercises

mixed practice

1. Pete – pet – pen – pan – pane – mane – mine

2. cube – cub – cob – cop – cope – cape – cake – take

3. role – mole – mule – male – tale – tile – pile

4. cut – cute – mute – mate – make – Mike – bike

5. pale – pile – pole – mole – mule – rule – rude

Sample Sound Board Exercises

(closed syllable and final "e" pairs with blends and digraphs)

a-e	*i-e*	*o-e*
bath → bathe	quit → quite	slop → slope
plan → plane	slid → slide	glob → globe
scrap → scrape	slim → slime	
	spit → spite	
	spin → spine	
	twin → twine	
	strip → stripe	

Yellow Level

Sample Sound Board Exercises

(*a-e* and *i-e* including blends and digraphs)

a-e

1. plan – plane – plate – state – stake – take
2. grade – grape – tape – tame – blame – flame – flake
3. tap – tape – ape – shape – shade – made – mad
4. pan – pane – plane – plan – can – cane – crane
5. man – mane – maze – blaze – blame – same – Sam
6. quake – brake – brave – crave – crane – crate – slate

i-e

1. Tim – time – lime – slime – slim – slid – slide
2. rid – ride – bride – glide – pride – prize
3. pin – pine – shine – fine – fin – spin – spine
4. thin – win – twin – twine – dine – dime – dim
5. quit – quite – bite – bit – spit – spite – spike
6. shin – shine – swine – swipe – stripe – strike – stride

Sample Sound Board Exercises

(*a-e* and *i-e, o-e,* and *u-e* including blends and digraphs)

a-e and i-e

1. smile – mile – male – stale – state – slate – slat

2. slide – slid – lid – lad – glad – glade - glide

3. slim – slime – time – tame – frame – lame - blame

o-e

1. cone – stone – stove – wove – woke – yoke – smoke

2. dove – drove – stove – stoke – broke – spoke – poke

3. prod – rod – rode – robe – globe – glob – snob

u-e

1. rule – mule – mute – flute – fluke – duke – dune

2. cute – cut – cub – cube – cute – flute - fluke

Road to Reading: A Program for Preventing and Remediating Reading Difficulties by Benita A. Blachman & Darlene M. Tangel

189

Sample Sound Board Exercises

(final "e" including blends and digraphs)

mixed practice

1. shine – shin – bin – bit – quit – quite – quote

2. tile – tale – stale – stole – mole – mile – smile

3. dove – dive – drive – drove – stove – Steve – eve

4. plan – pan – pin – pine – spine – spin

5. mat – mate – mute – flute – cute – cut

Sample Dictation Exercises

a-e

<table>
<tr><td>

_a_   **_a-e_**
mad   made
tap   tape
pan

Dave came to the lake.

</td><td>

_a-e_   **_a_**
gave   can
same   chap
       tab

Jake gave Jane a game.

</td></tr>
<tr><td>

_a-e_   **_a_**
tape   zap
cane   hat
lane

I will bake a cake.

</td><td>

_a_   **_a-e_**
pan   cape
cap   same
       base

Mom is late.

</td></tr>
</table>

_a_   **_a-e_**
rat   fake
       safe
       rate

Pam can wade in the lake.

Sample Dictation Exercises

i-e

i-e	***i***
file	thin
like	chin
tide	

I ran a mile.

i	***i-e***
win	pine
sip	ripe
	size

The bug will bite the cat.

a	***i***	***i-e***
math	rid	ride
	dim	dime

It is time to line up.

Sample Dictation Exercises

i-e

a	*a-e*	*i*	*i-e*
rash	ate	fib	bite
	make		side

That kite is mine.

a-e	*a*	*i-e*	*i*
vane	van	hide	fish
		fine	pig

I ate the ripe lime.

Sample Dictation Exercises

o-e

o-e	**o**
home	mom
zone	got
	shop

I can tell a joke.

o	**o-e**
mop	cone
job	mope
	lone

Sam dug a big hole.

i	**o**	**i-e**	**o-e**
kit	hop	kite	rode
	rock		hope

Tom ran nine miles.

a-e	**i-e**	**o**	**o-e**
take	tide	rob	vote
		cop	nope

The pole is in the hole.

Road to Reading: A Program for Preventing and Remediating Reading Difficulties by Benita A. Blachman & Darlene M. Tangel

Yellow Level

Sample Dictation Exercises

u-e

u	**u-e**
run	use
bug	cute
	mule

The mule ran up the hill.

o	**o-e**	**u**	**u-e**
mob	tote	rub	dude
		sum	tube

The dude is rude.

a-e	**o-e**	**u**	**u-e**
wake	woke	cub	cube
cave	rope		

June sat in the tube.

Sample Dictation Exercises

mixed practice

_a-e_	**_i-e_**	**_o-e_**
came	ride	lobe
late	bite	

The rose is in the vase.

_a-e_	**_u-e_**	**_e-e_**
late	fuse	eve
	tune	Pete

I will ride the mule.

_i-e_	**_i_**	**_o-e_**
pile	fit	mole
	wish	pole

Wipe up this mess!

Yellow Level

Sample Dictation Exercises

mixed practice

_a-e_	**_i_**	**_i-e_**	**_u-e_**
bake	kit	kite	rule
		life	mute

Pete dove in the lake.

_i_	**_i-e_**	**_o_**	**_o-e_**
sit	site	hot	cone
dim	dime		

Be home at nine.

_a-e_	**_o-e_**	**_u-e_**	**_e-e_**
late	joke	fuse	eve
		tune	Pete

The lame pig came home.

Yellow Level

Sample Dictation Exercises

(final "e" including blends and digraphs)

a-e

a	**a-e**
camp	brave
snack	plane
mad	

Get that snake!

a-e	**i-e**
shake	kite
late	ride
flake	

Tom skates on the lake.

a	**i**	**a-e**
band	snip	trade
	chin	stale

I ate the grape.

Sample Dictation Exercises

(final "e" including blends and digraphs)

i-e

_i-e_	**_i_**
slide	trip
mile	lid
chime	

I got the prize.

_i-e_	**_o-e_**
glide	bone
pine	rode
twine	

Kim sat in the slime.

_a_	**_i_**	**_i-e_**
stand	swim	bride
graph		pike

The sun will shine.

Yellow Level

Sample Dictation Exercises

(final "e" including blends and digraphs)

o-e

o-e	**o**
froze	spot
smoke	mop
choke	

Stan drove home.

a-e	**i-e**	**o-e**
frame	mine	phone
shade		spoke

I broke the lamp.

i	**o**	**i-e**	**o-e**
spin	drop	white	stone
		spine	grove

The pot is on the stove.

Yellow Level

Sample Dictation Exercises

(final "e" including blends and digraphs)

u-e

u	**u-e**
brush	fluke
cub	rule
	cube

The flute is mine.

u-e	**u**
rule	truck
tune	must
	slush

I can ride in the truck.

Sample Dictation Exercises

(final "e" including blends and digraphs)

mixed practice

a-e	**i-e**	**o-e**
made	drive	globe
brake		drove

Do not shake the slide.

a-e	**o-e**	**u-e**
cake	home	mule
skate	broke	

Steve drove a van.

a-e	**i-e**	**o-e**
cape	tribe	spoke
slate		froze

Tom will trade his prize.

Road to Reading: A Program for Preventing and Remediating Reading Difficulties by Benita A. Blachman & Darlene M. Tangel

-Green Level-

203

> **Please note:** The Green, Blue, and Purple levels will no longer provide a cumulative list of skills to review from the Red, Orange, and Yellow levels. Depending on the needs of individual students, you will need to spend more or less time reviewing previously taught skills. The progress notes that you make on your daily lesson plans should help you decide what needs to be reviewed.

Goals for the Green Level

When the students complete this level, they should be able to do the following:

 Read words with Group I vowel teams—*ee, oa, ai, ea, oe, ie, ay,* and *ow*—and single consonants (e.g., j<u>ee</u>p, c<u>oa</u>t, n<u>ai</u>l, s<u>ea</u>l, t<u>oe</u>, p<u>ie</u>, h<u>ay</u>, l<u>ow</u>).

 Read words with Group I vowel teams—*ee, oa, ai, ea, ay,* and *ow*—with digraphs and initial and final blends (e.g., sh<u>ee</u>p, fl<u>oa</u>t, st<u>ai</u>n, cl<u>ea</u>n, pr<u>ay</u>, sn<u>ow</u>).

 Read words with Group II vowel teams—*ou, oo, ow, aw, au, oi, oy, ew,* and *ea*—with single consonants (e.g., <u>ou</u>t, m<u>oo</u>n, b<u>oo</u>k, c<u>ow</u>, p<u>aw</u>, h<u>au</u>l, c<u>oi</u>n, j<u>oy</u>, n<u>ew</u>, h<u>ea</u>d).

 Read words with Group II vowel teams—*ou, oo, ow, aw, au, oi, oy, ew,* and *ea*—with digraphs and initial and final blends (e.g., sc<u>ou</u>t, sch<u>oo</u>l, br<u>oo</u>k, pl<u>ow</u>, cr<u>aw</u>l, <u>Au</u>gust, sp<u>oi</u>l, pl<u>oy</u>, ch<u>ew</u>, br<u>ea</u>d).

 Read selected contractions made up of simple closed syllables (e.g., *did not* becomes *did<u>n't</u>*) and open and closed syllables (e.g., *she is* becomes *sh<u>e's</u>*).

Read words with the *-igh(t)* pattern (e.g., s**igh**, n**ight**, flash-l**ight**).

 Read two-syllable words with a vowel between two consonants (e.g., *robot, limit*).

 Read two-syllable words made up of closed, final "e," open, and vowel team syllables (e.g., *napkin, pancake, invite, peanut, sailboat, tiptoe, robot*).

Step 1

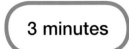

3 minutes

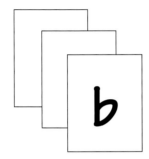

Review Sound–Symbol Correspondences

Materials

Sound pack cards (sounds for review and new sounds)

Procedures

Use your sound pack of previously learned letters to quickly review the letter names and sounds with your students. Remember, the goal is to develop fluency, not boredom.

You will not need to continue to review all of the consonants at this point. You should, however, continue to review any consonants and digraphs (*th, ch, sh, wh, ph,* and *-ck*) that the students do not know automatically, as well as the five short vowels and final "e" graphemes (e.g., *a-e*).

To facilitate teaching the vowel teams, we have divided the vowel teams into two groups. The groups are somewhat arbitrary. You will notice that in Group I the vowel teams retain the sound of the first letter. Group II vowel teams make a new sound and may have more than one sound.

Please note: We have only included the vowel teams that have the highest frequency and regularity in the language and, thus, the greatest utility. We did not include, for example, the vowel team *ui* because we have found that there are so few words that contain this vowel team (e.g., *s<u>ui</u>t, fr<u>ui</u>t*). It is easier to teach these words as sight words.

You should feel free, however, to introduce additional vowel teams that appear in the materials your students are reading, regardless of whether they are included in our lists.

To help the students learn the Group I vowel teams—*ee* (e.g., *j<u>ee</u>p*), *oa* (e.g., *c<u>oa</u>t*), *ai* (e.g., *sn<u>ai</u>l*), *ea* (e.g., *s<u>ea</u>l*), *oe* (e.g., *t<u>oe</u>*), *ie* (e.g., *p<u>ie</u>*), *ay* (e.g., *h<u>ay</u>*), and *ow* (e.g., *l<u>ow</u>*)—gradually add the vowel teams to the sound pack as each one is introduced.

Group II Vowel Teams

To help the students learn the Group II vowel teams—*ou* (e.g., sc*ou*t), *oo* (e.g., sch*oo*l, b*oo*k), *ow* (e.g., pl*ow*), *aw* (e.g., l*aw*n), *au* (e.g., *Au*gust), *oi* (e.g., c*oi*n), *oy* (e.g., j*oy*), *ew* (e.g., fl*ew*), and *ea* (e.g., br*ea*d)—gradually add the vowel teams to the sound pack as each one is introduced.

Students should be able to give two sounds for *oo* (as in sch*oo*l and b*oo*k), two sounds for *ow* (as in sn*ow* and pl*ow*), and two sounds for *ea* (as in s*ea*l and br*ea*d). (The /ow/ sound in sn*ow* and the /ea/ sound in s*ea*l were introduced in Group I vowel teams).

When the students have been taught both sounds for each vowel team, put two dots in the upper right corner of the /oo/ sound card, the /ow/ sound card, and the /ea/ sound card to help the students remember to give both sounds.

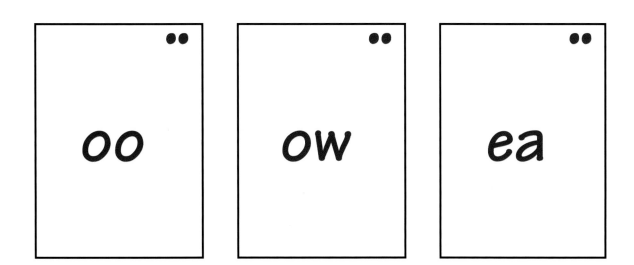

Step 2

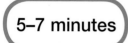

Teach or Review New Decoding Skill

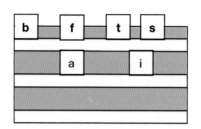

Step 2

5–7 minutes

Materials

 Sound board for each student

 Consonant letters and digraphs in the top pocket (only include those needed to make words for a particular lesson)

 Vowel letters and vowel teams in the middle pocket (only include those needed to make words for a particular lesson)

Procedures

The order of introduction of the vowel teams is relatively consistent with the order of introduction of these vowel teams in the Green Level decodable book chart.

Feel free to alter the order of introduction of the vowel teams to match the order of introduction of the vowel teams in whichever reading materials you are using.

Group I Vowel Teams

Use the sound board to introduce the Group I vowel teams: *ee* (e.g., *j**ee**p*), *oa* (e.g., *c**oa**t*), *ai* (e.g., *n**ai**l*), *ea* (e.g., *s**ea**l*), *oe* (e.g., *t**oe***), *ie* (e.g., *p**ie***), *ay* (e.g., *h**ay***), and *ow* (e.g., *l**ow***).

> Occasionally you will see a word on our sample sound board lists referred to as a "challenge word." A few examples will appear on yellow notes. If you feel that one or more of the students in your group is ready, include a challenge word in your lesson. You can give the word to an individual student or to the whole group.

A sound board list might look like the following (read across):

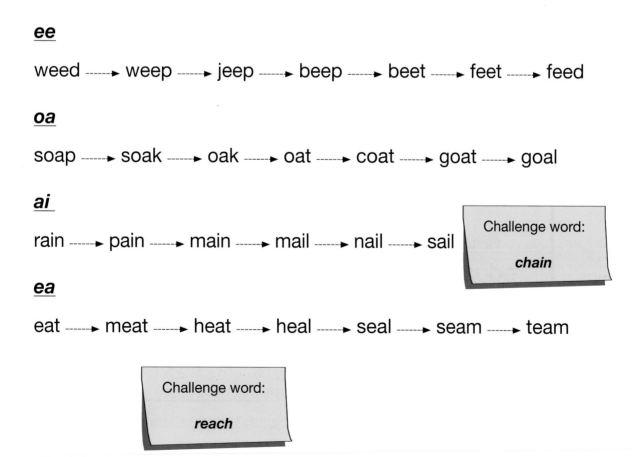

ee

weed ------► weep ------► jeep ------► beep ------► beet ------► feet ------► feed

oa

soap ------► soak ------► oak ------► oat ------► coat ------► goat ------► goal

ai

rain ------► pain ------► main ------► mail ------► nail ------► sail

Challenge word:

chain

ea

eat ------► meat ------► heat ------► heal ------► seal ------► seam ------► team

Challenge word:

reach

oe and ie

tie ------> toe ------> doe ------> die ------> pie ------> lie

> **Please note:** In the *ay* and *ai* list below, the students will have two vowel team cards on their sound board. These vowel teams—*ay* and *ai*—make the same sound. Point out to the students that *ay* always goes at the end of a word or syllable, whereas *ai* goes in the middle of a one-syllable word.

Step 2

ay and ai

lay ------> ray ------> pay ------> paid ------> laid ------> lay ------> may ------> maid

ow

row ------> low ------> tow ------> mow ------> bow ------> bowl

Now that the students can make words with Group I vowel teams with single consonants on the sound board, use the sound board to demonstrate what happens when you add blends and digraphs to these vowel team words. For example, have students make the following words:

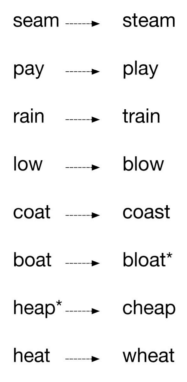

*Do your students know what a **heap** is?

If not, this is a good opportunity to expand their vocabulary.

seam ----→ steam

pay ----→ play

rain ----→ train

low ----→ blow

coat ----→ coast

boat ----→ bloat*

heap* ----→ cheap

heat ----→ wheat

*Do your students know what the word **bloat** means?

Remember to look for other opportunities to extend vocabulary in each lesson.

Step 2

You may need to make the first word (e.g., *seam*) and then ask the students to make it into the second word (e.g., *steam*).

Once the students can make **pairs** with the blends, you can go back to making sound board **lists** and changing one sound at a time. ***It is okay to change two sounds if you are making a word with a blend, such as <u>st</u>ain, into a word without a blend, such as <u>g</u>ain.***

For example (read across):

pain ----→ stain ----→ gain ----→ grain ----→ groan ----→ green ----→ teen

You can make this activity more challenging by adding words with three-letter blends (e.g., making *seam* ------▶ *steam* ------▶ *stream* or *rain* ------▶ *train* ------▶ *strain*).

See the Additional Materials section at the end of this level for more sample sound board exercises for words with Group I vowel teams and lists of words with three-letter blends.

Group II Vowel Teams

Step 2

Use the sound board to introduce the Group II vowel teams—*ou* (e.g., sc<u>ou</u>t), *oo* (e.g., sch<u>oo</u>l, b<u>oo</u>k), *ow* (e.g., pl<u>ow</u>), *aw* (e.g., l<u>aw</u>n), *au* (e.g., **A**<u>u</u>gust), *oi* (e.g., c<u>oi</u>n), *oy* (e.g., j<u>oy</u>), *ew* (e.g., fl<u>ew</u>), and *ea* (e.g., br<u>ea</u>d)—with single consonants, digraphs, and initial and final blends.

> ***Please note:*** Once most students are ready to learn the Group II vowel teams, they no longer need the vowel teams to be introduced initially with only single consonants. Therefore, the lists that follow include the Group II vowel teams with single consonants, digraphs, and initial and final blends. ***Some of the more challenging lists may also require up to three sound changes as new words are made.***
>
> If you have students who initially have difficulty making words with Group II vowel teams and digraphs and/or blends on the sound board, restrict your first lists to words with single consonants. Then, gradually add the digraphs and blends.

A sound board list might look like the following (read across):

_ou_

out ---→ shout ---→ south ---→ mouth ---→ mound ---→ mount ---→ count

_oo_

boom ---→ broom ---→ groom ---→ groan ---→ moan ---→ moon ---→
smooth

_oo_

brook ---→ book ---→ beak ---→ sneak ---→ shook ---→ crook ---→ cook

_ow_

cow ---→ chow ---→ howl ---→ down ---→ drown ---→ drain ---→ chain

_aw_

raw ---→ draw ---→ claw ---→ clay ---→ play ---→ paw ---→ straw

_au_

Paul ---→ haul ---→ haunt ---→ hunt ---→ hunch ---→ lunch ---→ launch

_oi_

oil ---→ spoil ---→ point ---→ moist ---→ mist ---→ brisk ---→ broil

_oy_

boy ---→ Roy ---→ ray ---→ tray ---→ joy ---→ jay

Remember, some
words require three
sound changes as
new words are made.

Step
2

_ew_

new ---→ few ---→ stew ---→ flew ---→ crew ---→ crown ---→ clown

_ea_

read ---→ bread ---→ spread ---→ sprout* ---→ sprain* ---→ grain ---→
grown

> *Do your students know what the words **sprout** and **sprain** mean?
>
> Remember to look for opportunities to extend vocabulary in each lesson.

Step
2

See the Additional Materials section at the end of this level for additional sound board sample exercises for Group II vowel teams.

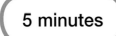

Step 3

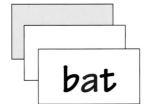

bat

Review Phonetically Regular Words (PRWs) and High Frequency Words (HFWs)

Materials

Phonetically regular word (PRW) cards (only those words you plan to use in a particular lesson)

High frequency word (HFW) cards (only those words that you plan to use in a particular lesson)

One dry erase board, one dry erase marker, and one eraser for the teacher

Procedures

The goal of this activity is to develop fluency. The focus is on the phonetically regular words, with a few high frequency words included.

The phonetically regular words (PRWs) should consist of words with the new patterns you are teaching (Group I and Group II vowel teams with single consonants, digraphs, and initial and final blends).

Step
3

Words with previously learned syllable patterns (e.g., closed, open, and final "e" syllables) should also be included in your word cards and reviewed.

> You may want to increase the number of words you have in your word cards. If you included 12 phonetically regular words and 3 high frequency words in previous lessons, you might consider increasing the number to include 15 phonetically regular words and 5 high frequency words.
>
> Remember that the phonetically regular words (PRWs) and high frequency words (HFWs) should be written on different colored cards. For example, you might choose to write the PRWs on white cards and the HFWs on yellow cards.

Phonetically Regular Words (PRWs)

Group I Vowel Team Words

- Once the students can successfully make words with the first Group I vowel team *ee* and single consonants (e.g., *jeep*) on the sound board, you can add words with *ee* to your phonetically regular word (PRW) cards and introduce words with *oa* and single consonants on the sound board.

- Follow the same procedure with the other Group I vowel teams and single consonants (e.g., *oa* as in *coat*, *ai* as in *nail*, *ea* as in *seal*, *oe* as in *toe*, *ie* as in *pie*, *ay* as in *hay*, *ow* as in *low*), adding words with these patterns to the phonetically regular word (PRW) cards once students can make these words on the sound board.

- Once the students can successfully make words with the Group I vowel team *ee* and blends and digraphs (e.g., s*ee*p) on the sound board, you can add words with *ee* and blends and digraphs to your phonetically regular word cards and introduce words with *oa* and blends and digraphs on the sound board.

- Follow the same procedure with other Group I vowel teams and blends and digraphs (e.g., *oa* as in f*oa*t, *ai* as in sn*ai*l, *ea* as in pr*ea*ch, *ay* as in st*ay*, *ow* as in sn*ow*), adding words with these patterns to the phonetically regular word cards once students can make these words on the sound board.

A starter set of PRW words for the Group I vowel teams is provided on the next page. The Additional Materials section at the end of this level includes additional lists of Group I vowel team words with single consonants and with digraphs and blends.

Starter Set of Green Level Phonetically Regular Word (PRW) Cards

Group I vowel teams with single consonants

ee	**oa**	**ai**	**ea**	**oe**
feed	boat	rain	beat	Joe
keep	coat	pain	deal	toe
seem	goat	nail	eat	hoe
peek	road	tail	meat	doe
week	load	wait	heat	foe
	soap		seat	
			team	
			read	
			sea	

ie	**ay**	**ow**
pie	way	tow
tie	may	mow
lie	day	
die	lay	
	say	

Group I vowel teams with digraphs and blends

ee	**oa**	**ai**	**ea**	**ay**	**ow**
sheep	float	claim	flea	play	slow
free	croak	chain	clean	tray	blow
creep		stain	cheat		grow
tree					show

When you add these words to your phonetically regular word (PRW) cards, remember to write the consonants in black and the vowel teams in red.

You can make Step 3 more challenging by adding words with -ed endings (e.g., heat**ed**, sail**ed**, peek**ed**) and by adding words with three-letter blends (e.g., **str**eam, **spr**ay) to your PRW cards with Group I vowel teams. See the Additional Materials section at the end of this level for lists of words with -ed endings and words with three-letter blends.

Group II Vowel Team Words

- Once the students can successfully make words with the first Group II vowel team *ou* and single consonants, digraphs, and initial and final blends (e.g., sc**ou**t) on the sound board, you can add words with *ou* and digraphs and blends to your phonetically regular word (PRW) cards and introduce words with *oo* and single consonants, digraphs, and initial and final blends (e.g., sch**oo**l, b**oo**k) on the sound board.

- Follow the same procedure with the other Group II vowel teams and single consonants, digraphs, and initial and final blends (e.g., *oo* as in sch**oo**l and b**oo**k, *ow* as in sn**ow** and pl**ow**, *aw* as in l**aw**n, *au* as in **Au**gust, *oi* as in c**oi**n, *oy* as in j**oy**, *ew* as in fl**ew**, *ea* as in s**ea**l and br**ea**d), adding words with these patterns to the phonetically regular word (PRW) cards once students can make these words on the sound board.

A starter set of Group II PRWs is provided on the next page. The Additional Materials section at the end of this level includes additional lists of Group II vowel team words. Use blank white cards to add to the starter set as the students learn more words. Remember to write the vowel teams in red.

Starter Set of Green Level Phonetically Regular Word (PRW) Cards

Group II vowel teams with single consonants, digraphs, and blends

ou	**oo**	**oo**	**ow**	**aw**
out	fool	cook	cow	saw
ouch	tool	foot	now	claw
mouth	pool	book	wow	paw
shout	loop	took	town	raw
couch	food	wood	down	draw
count	zoo	wool	gown	lawn
loud	roof	good	chow	jaw
	mood	hook		law
	room	hood		

au	**oi**	**oy**	**ew**	**ea**
Paul	boil	toy	new	head
haul	coin	boy	blew	bread
maul	soil	Roy	flew	sweat
	foil	soy	few	spread
	oil		crew	breadth
	join		drew	health

Words with Contractions (Minilesson)

It is helpful to introduce the concept of contractions in Step 3 of the lesson.

- Write both words (e.g., *it is*) on the dry erase board.

- Show the students how you can shorten these words by erasing one or more letters from the second word and adding an apostrophe where the letters were erased.

- Point out to the students that the first word almost always remains intact.

- In the list below, read the first pair for the students. Have the students read the remaining pairs.

Make the following words into contractions using the procedure described above:

he	is	----→	he's
she	is	----→	she's
it	is	----→	it's
did	not	----→	didn't
can	not	----→	can't
I	will	----→	I'll

> ***Please note:*** We are only creating contractions from phonetically regular words that the students have learned how to decode in this or previous levels of the program. We are not including contractions that use high frequency words (e.g., *you have* becomes *you've*). Once the students understand the basic concept of contractions, these more complex contractions can be introduced as the students encounter them in their reading.

Words with the -igh(t) Pattern (a Special Case)

It also is a good idea to introduce the *-igh(t)* pattern in this step of the lesson.

Introduce the *-igh(t)* pattern by writing the following words on **your** dry erase board:

h<u>igh</u>

s<u>igh</u>

- Underline the *-igh* in each word, and tell the students that this letter combination makes the long /i/ sound.

- Read each word for the students, and ask them to repeat the word after you.

- Ask the students if they hear the sounds of the letters *g* and *h*. Tell the students that these letters are silent.

- Erase the word *high*—but keep the word *sigh*—on the dry erase board. Show the students that by adding *t* to *sigh*, *sigh* becomes *sight*. Remind them that the *g* and the *h* are silent.

- Using the list below, show the students how you can make additional words with the *-igh(t)* pattern by changing the first letter of the word *sight* on the dry erase board. Have the students read each new word as you make it.

right	might
night	flight
tight	fright
light	bright
fight	

Once students can read words with the *-ight* pattern, show them that words with this pattern can also be used in compound words.

Write the following words on the dry erase board:

flashlight

streetlight

sunlight

nightlight

- Read the first word for the students.

- Ask for volunteers to read each of the remaining words.

- If the students have trouble reading the words, separate each compound word by writing the words separately on the dry erase board or by writing each word on an individual card (as you did in previous levels), and have the students read each of the individual words before putting the compound word together.

- Next, physically move the cards together and have the students read the word.

Include words with the *-igh(t)* pattern in your phonetically regular word (PRW) cards.

Step
3

Compound Words

Groups Moving Quickly

For groups moving quickly, continue to introduce compound words made up of the syllable types the students have already learned (i.e., closed, final "e," and Group I and Group II vowel teams), such as *raincoat, tiptoe*, *peanut*, and *mailbox*.

Because blends and digraphs are being added to vowel team syllables in this level, blends and digraphs can also be added to compound words that include these syllable types (e.g., *snowflake, coastline*, *paintbrush*).

Students moving quickly can be given the opportunity to read many compound words in this step. Compound words can be put on white index cards for review, just as you do with any other phonetically regular words in this step.

Groups Needing More Practice

You may be introducing compound words for the first time to some groups. If this is the case, refer to the Compound Word section of Step 3 of the Yellow Level for suggested activities and examples for teaching simple compound words such as *sunset* and *backpack*.

Once students can read compound words using only closed syllables, introduce words using closed syllables and final "e" syllables (e.g., *pancake*) and then words with vowel teams (e.g., *mailbox*).

The number of compound words that you include in this step will depend on the group's accuracy and fluency with one-syllable words.

Two-Syllable Words (such as *robot, limit*)

> ***Please note:*** For two-syllable words with one consonant between two vowels (e.g., *robot, limit*), the word is divided in one of two ways. Sometimes it is divided after the first vowel (e.g., **ro**/*bot*) and the first syllable is open. Other times it is divided after the consonant (e.g., **lim**/*it*) and the first syllable is closed.
>
> If students are still having difficulty with two-syllable words with simpler constructions, such as *pancake, toenail, rabbit,* and *mitten,* feel free to delay introducing this concept until Step 3 of the next level—the Blue Level.

To introduce students to the two-syllable words with one consonant between two vowels, we have provided three lists for practice:

1. The first list contains words that should be divided after the vowel (e.g., *ro/bot*).

2. The second list contains words that should be divided after the consonant (e.g., *lim/it*).

3. The third and final list provides mixed practice (e.g., *ro/bot, lim/it*).

Two-Syllable Words Divided After the Vowel

To introduce two-syllable words with one consonant between two vowels, write the following words on your dry erase board and divide them **after** the first vowel:

> ro/bot
>
> e/ven
>
> he/ro
>
> o/pen
>
> hu/man
>
> de/pend
>
> si/lent
>
> re/lax
>
> so/lo
>
> mi/nus

- Remind the students that when the word is divided after the vowel, the vowel will have the long sound (says the vowel's name). This is an open syllable. (The students were introduced to simple open syllable words, e.g., *he*, *go*, and *my* in the Yellow Level.)

- Demonstrate dividing and reading the word *ro/bot*.

- Ask the students to read the rest of the words on the list, making sure that they give the long sound for the first vowel.

Two-Syllable Words Divided After the Consonant

The following day, continue to review this syllable division concept by writing the following words on your dry erase board. Divide these words **after** the consonant:

> lim/it
>
> hab/it
>
> rob/in
>
> men/u
>
> vis/it
>
> cab/in
>
> plan/et

- Remind the students that when they divide after the consonant, the vowel will have the short sound. This is a closed syllable. (If you have not yet introduced the term *closed syllable* to the students, you might want to introduce it now. Remember, a closed syllable has one vowel and ends in one or more consonants. The vowel says its short sound, as in *it, fun*, and *splash.*)

- Demonstrate dividing and reading the word *lim/it*.

- Ask the students to read the rest of the words you have written on the dry erase board, making sure that they give the short sound for the first vowel.

Two-Syllable Words, Mixed Practice

For mixed practice, write the following words on the dry erase board. This list may be more difficult for the students because they will have to decide if the word should be divided after either the vowel or the consonant.

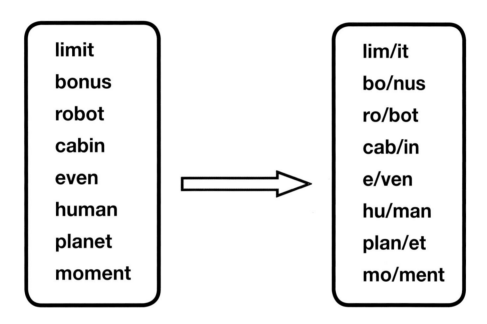

limit	lim/it
bonus	bo/nus
robot	ro/bot
cabin	cab/in
even	e/ven
human	hu/man
planet	plan/et
moment	mo/ment

- Have a student divide the word *limit.*

- If the student divides it correctly (i.e., *lim/it*), have the student read the word.

- If the student divides it incorrectly (i.e., *li/mit*), ask the student to read the first syllable. As divided, it is an open syllable, so the vowel will have the long sound (say its name).

- Have the student read the second syllable and then read the whole word.

- Ask the student if *li/mit* is a real word ("Does it sound like a word you've heard before?").

- Next, show the student that if you move the dividing line after the consonant (i.e., *lim/it*), then you have the real word *limit* with two closed syllables.

- Follow the same procedure for the remaining words on the list.

- Divide each word and then have the student read the word.

High Frequency Words (HFWs) 151–200

The following high frequency words (HFWs) from Fry and Kress (2006) can be taught and added to your word card pack. You might want to pretest the students on these HFWs at this level and create an individualized list of HFWs that the students still need to learn. A High Frequency Word Assessment form for the Green Level and individual word cards are included on the CD-ROM.

*set	put	*end	does	another	*well	large
*must	*big	**even	*such	because	turn	here
*why	*ask	*went	*men	**read	**need	*land
different	*home	*us	move	*try	kind	*hand
picture	again	change	off	**play	*spell	air
away	animal	house	**point	page	letter	mother
answer	**found	study	*still	learn	should	America
world						

Adapted from *The Reading Teacher's Book of Lists, Fifth Edition,* by E.B. Fry and J. Kress
© 2006 Jossey-Bass. Reprinted with permission from John Wiley & Sons, Inc.

*Students learned to decode words written in red, orange, and **yellow** during the Red, Orange, and **Yellow** levels in this program, respectively.

**Students will be learning to decode the words written in green at this level in the program.

Once each high frequency word has been mastered by most of the students, you might want to file the word in alphabetical order in the back of a high frequency word box. These words should be reviewed on a regular basis in Step 3 of your lesson to make sure that the students remember them.

As is evident from the many high frequency words (HFWs) in the Green Level that appear color-coded in the chart on the previous page, students who have learned the four syllable types presented thus far can use their decoding skills to read about half of the high frequency words included in this level. This greatly reduces the number of HFWs that might otherwise need to be memorized.

An Important Note About Developing Fluency

Remember, the overall goal of this activity is to develop fluency at the word level. A hallmark of good readers is the ability to read both accurately and fluently.

To help students develop fluency, you will need to have them read the words more than once. The first time the words are read, the goal is accuracy. If a student misreads a vowel or vowel team in a word, it helps to point to the vowel or vowel team and ask the student to tell you the sound the vowel or vowel team makes. Then, ask the student to read the entire word. If the student continues to read the word incorrectly, then pronounce the word for the student and move on.

Activities for Developing Fluency

- When the students read the words for the second time, try using an hourglass to encourage the students to move more quickly. The students like to see how many words they can read before the sand runs out.

- Use a stopwatch with the students and have the students see how long it takes to read all the words in the card pack for that day. As you go around the group, you can accommodate a student who reads less fluently by asking that student to read a word that you know he or she can read. This ensures that each student gets a turn and keeps the activity moving.

- Students can also use the hourglass and stopwatch while working in pairs. Each student tries to read his or her words more quickly than during his or her previous reading. This way, the students are encouraged to improve their own times and not compete with each other.

Step 4 Read Orally in Context

Materials

Selected decodable readers (see Green Level chart)

Selected books/stories from your classroom or school library or basal program (suggested book titles appear in Appendix B)

Procedures

Please note: The amount of time suggested for oral reading has been increased an additional 5 minutes to 15–20 minutes in this level. Students should be reading more connected text, and adequate time needs to be allocated for that practice.

You may find that on some days you can spend less time on other steps to gain additional minutes for oral reading. For example, on a day when you are not adding anything new to the sound board in Step 2 or on a day when you are not adding any new pattern to the word cards in Step 3, you may be able to spend less time on those steps and more time on oral reading.

It is also important that students have opportunities to read orally with corrective feedback at other times during the day.

> Remember that all time guidelines given are only suggestions to help plan each lesson. Times need to be adjusted (up or down) for each step, depending on the needs of your students.

In this section, we list a variety of options for reading material. The choices you make will depend on the skill level of the students in your group.

We encourage you to reread familiar books with all of your students to develop oral reading fluency. As noted in the *Report of the National Reading Panel* (National Institute of Child Health and Human Development, 2000), "Fluent readers are able to read orally with speed, accuracy, and proper expression. Fluency is one of several critical factors for reading comprehension" (p. 11).

Step
4

Decodable Book Chart for the Green Level

To help you select books for your groups, we have created decodable book charts for the first five levels of this program.

Books on this chart are arranged by the vowel team patterns being taught in this level.

This chart is meant to help you individualize instruction for your students. ***Remember, other decodable books may be substituted for those on the chart.***

There will be a great deal of variation in the number of decodable books that each student needs to read. Some students may continue to need to read ***many*** highly decodable readers, such as those on the chart, to reinforce the patterns they are learning and to become accurate and fluent readers. Other students at this level will be much more independent and will be able to read a much wider variety of carefully selected materials, such as chapter books, nonfiction, poetry, and plays.

Although these books are highly decodable (phonetically regular), each book also introduces a small number of high frequency words not previously introduced in this program; these words are also included on the chart.

If a phonetically regular word appears on the chart, it signals that that pattern has not been taught ***yet*** in this program.

Green Level Decodable Book Chart

SV = Steck-Vaughn

PP = Primary Phonics
MPP = More Primary Phonics

			Decodable Books with Vowel Teams		
		Title	**Vowel**	**New Words***	**Ending**
1	PP 2-5	*The Bee*	ee	doe, toe, pie	
2	PP 2-6	*The Goat*	oa		
3	SV 2-7	*Mole King Cole and Anna Tole*	oa	king, old, Anna	
4	SV 2-1	*A Race on the Lake*	ai	pulls	's
5	SV 2-2	*The Cake Bake*	ai	puts, out	's
6	PP 2-7	*Sail*	oa, ai		
7	MPP M2-7	*Cop Cat and the Mule*	oa, ai	tied	
8	MPP M2-6	*A Fine Coat*	ee, oa, ai	nice	
9	PP 2-8	*The Seal*	ee, ea		
10	MPP M2-8	*A Real Pal*	oa, ai, ea		
11	PP 2-9	*Hide and Seek*	ee, ea	lie, Joe	
12	MPP M2-9	*Rose and Weed*	ee, ea		
13	SV 2-10	*Hide and Seek*	ee, ea	leaves	
14	PP 2-10	*The Fire*	ee, oa, ai, ea		
15	MPP M2-5	*The Lie*	ee, oe, ie	saw	
16	SV 2-9	*A Real Seal*	ee, ea, oe	way, arr (seal sound), meow	's
17	MPP M2-10	*The Deer*	ai, ea, ee, oa, ie		
18	PP 3-1	*Slide*	a-e, i-e, o-e, ee, ai		
19	PP 3-4	*The Prints*	e-e, i-e, oa, ai, ea		
20	PP 3-5	*The Dream*	e-e, ai, ee, ea, ie		
21	PP 3-2	*The Plane Trip*	a-e, i-e, ee, ai, ea, ie		

Step

4

		Title	Vowel	New Words*	Ending
		Decodable Books with Vowel Teams			
22	PP 3-3	*Spot*	*a-e, o-e, e-e, ee, ea*		
23	PP 3-6	*The Best Gift*	*o-e, e-e, ee, ai, ie*		
24	PP 3-8	*The Sea Gull*	*e-e, oa, ea*		
25	SV 2-8	*Jo's Toes*	*oe*		
26	PP 3-9	*The Lost Duck*	*e-e, ea*	*cricket, racket*	
27	PP 3-7	*Mittens*	*a-e, ai, ee, ea*	*blanket, fireman, upstairs*	
28	PP 3-10	*Max and the Fox*	*o-e, e-e, ee, ea*		
29	PP 4-1	*Fish Fun*	*a-e, o-e, e-e, ee*	*out*	
30	PP 4-2	*The Chicken Ranch*	*a-e, o-e, e-e, ee, ea*	*sold*	
31	PP 4-3	*Ring the Bell*	*a-e, o-e, ee, ai, ea*	*hang, bang, rang*	
32	PP 4-5	*The White Hen*	*i-e, o-e, ee, ie*	*drink, out, upstairs*	
33	PP 5-1	*The Pet Poodle*	*oo* (as in sch**oo**l)	*forgot, sink, tore, jar, hard, torn*	
34	PP 5-2	*The Good Cook*	*oo* (as in b**oo**k)	*afternoon, hard, stir, store*	
35	PP 5-3	*Snow Fun*	*oo* (as in sch**oo**l and b**oo**k)	*middle, marshmallows, harder, tried, hurt, cried*	
36	PP 5-4	*A Cow in Town*	*oo, ow* (as in pl**ow**)	*near, Howard, farmer, sink, tried, owner, prowlers, flowers, cried,*	
37	PP 5-6	*The Shy Tiger*	*oo, ow*	*valley, monkey, tiger, scare, butterfly, cried*	
38	PP 5-5	*The Mouse House*	*ou, oo, ow*	*counter, sort*	
39	PP 5-9	*The Square Egg*	*ou, oo, ow*	*square, birthday, flutter, quiet, quickly, after, sort, yard, quarter, hear*	

*The *New Words* category in the decodable book chart includes both high frequency words that have not been taught yet in this program and phonetically regular words with patterns that have not been taught yet.

An Important Note About Building Fluency

Although many of your students will be becoming more fluent as they progress through the levels of the program, others will still require opportunities for ***frequent repeated readings*** of text with corrective feedback to continue to build fluency.

In addition to the list of texts provided, we have also provided Sample Reading Sentences in the Additional Materials section at the end of this level for further practice of all Group I and Group II vowel teams. Review previous suggestions in the Orange Level for ways to use these sentences.

Additional opportunities for repeated reading can occur by putting completed books in a center where students can reread them at other times during the day. This should not, however, replace repeated reading with corrective feedback by the teacher because repeated reading with corrective feedback has been found to be the most effective method for developing fluency.

An Important Note About Selecting Books

In addition to reading decodable books, students at this level should also have opportunities to read from a variety of other texts.

As mentioned previously, there will be a great deal of variation in the number of decodable books that students need to read.

Many students may be proficient enough to read most of the text in carefully selected trade books, such as chapter books, nonfiction, poetry, and plays. Other students may continue to need more support from the teacher (e.g., needing the teacher to supply unknown words or alternating reading when texts become longer, as in chapter books).

Appendix B contains some titles of trade books that many students will be able to read successfully. *Again, feel free to substitute your favorite books for students reading at this level.*

Step 5   Dictation

5–7 minutes

Materials

Dictation notebook for each student

Pencil

One dry erase board, one dry erase marker, and one eraser for the teacher

Procedures

• Each dictation exercise should include five or six words and one sentence that uses words with the same phonetic pattern.

• At the beginning of each notebook dictation session, ask the students to put the date on the top of that day's page.

• Tell the students which vowels they will be using for that day's lesson. These vowels will be their column headings.

• Have the students write the vowel headings on their page to help organize the dictation.

Once the students have set up the paper for that day's dictation, review the sounds of the vowels in the vowel headings before dictating the first word.

- Have the students write each word under the appropriate vowel as the word is dictated.

- The sound pack vowel cards from Step 1 corresponding to the vowels that you are using in dictation can be placed on the table as a reference for the students.

Once students can successfully make words with Group I vowel teams with single consonants, blends and digraphs (e.g., *pain, speed, coach*) on the sound board and you have included that pattern in other steps of the lesson, you are ready to include words with that pattern in dictation.

Likewise, once students can successfully make words with Group II vowel teams with single consonants, blends, and digraphs (e.g., *boy, flew, shout*) on the sound board and you have included that pattern in other steps of the lesson, you are ready to include words with that pattern in dictation.

If your group is ready to write a compound word (e.g., *tiptoe, clambake, coastline, toothbrush*), explain to the students that that word will **not** go under one of the vowel headings. That word can be a challenge word that is written on a separate line (not using the headings) before you dictate the sentence (see example on page 246). You can also use a compound word in the sentence if your group is reading these words correctly in Step 3.

> **Please note:** Although students have been introduced to other two-syllable words for reading (e.g., *rabbit, napkin, robot, limit*), *only* compound words should be used as challenge words in dictation at this level.

Group I Vowel Teams

In this level, focus the dictation exercises on Group I and Group II vowel teams with single consonants, blends, and digraphs.

Examples of notebook dictation pages: Group I vowel teams

<u>e</u>	<u>ee</u>
ten	teen
shed	jeep
	bee

The jeep is red.

<u>ai</u>	<u>oa</u>	<u>ea</u>
rain	boat	leap
pail	coat	

Jan ran to get a coat.

or

Jan ran to get a raincoat.

*raincoat (This might be a challenge word for your group. Include this word if you decide the students are ready for it.)

As students learn more vowel teams, include them in the dictation.

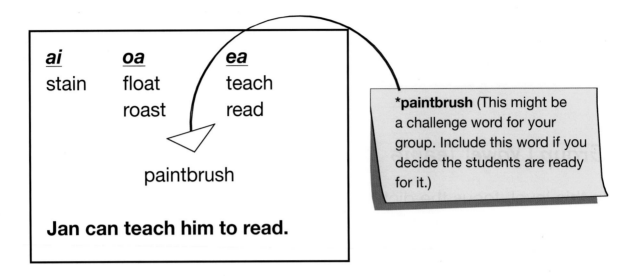

ai
stain

oa
float
roast

ea
teach
read

paintbrush

Jan can teach him to read.

*paintbrush (This might be a challenge word for your group. Include this word if you decide the students are ready for it.)

Step 5

- Check each student's work and help him or her correct errors.

- If the student continues to have difficulty, demonstrate for the student on *your* dry erase board, have the student copy the word correctly, and move on to the next word.

Group II Vowel Teams

As students learn Group II vowel teams, include words with these patterns in the dictation.

> **Please note:** Some of the Group II vowel teams make more than one sound (e.g., *oo* as in *school* and *book*). Remember to dictate words with only *one* of these sounds in a given lesson.

Examples of notebook dictation pages: Group II vowel teams

---

ou	**oa**	**o**
out	float	shop
south	soap	lock

The birds fly south.

---

oo	**aw**	**ow**
scoop	draw	cow
	crawl	clown

The toothbrush is in the bathroom.

- Again, check each student's work and help him or her correct errors.

- If the student continues to have difficulty, demonstrate for the student on *your* dry erase board, have the student copy the word correctly, and move on to the next word.

Refer to the Additional Materials section at the end of this level for more sample dictation exercises.

Step 5

If you are working with more advanced students and would like more challenging sentences for dictation, try dictating some of the Green Level Sample Reading Sentences found in the Additional Materials section at the end of this level.

You can vary the format when using these sentences by sending one student to the board to write the dictated sentence and having the other students provide corrective feedback, if necessary. You can also use the dry erase board and select one student to write the dictated sentence. After critiquing the sentence, you or the student can select the next student to use the dry erase board to write the next dictated sentence.

Additional Materials

Green Level

Phonetically Regular Word Lists

(Group I vowel teams: *ee* and *oa*)

ee			oa	
feed	deep		toad	coal
meet	beet		moan	loaf
beef	week		goal	soak
jeep	seed		road	foam
feel	peek		soap	oat
need	weep		loan	goat
seen	feet		oak	coat
keep	reel		load	
seem	bee			
eel	peel			

Compound words	*Compound words*
beehive	coatrack
	soapsuds

Green Level

Phonetically Regular Word Lists

(Group I vowel teams: *ai* and *ea*)

ai	
tail	jail
paid	bait
main	sail
nail	pail
rain	pain
laid	fail
aid	maid
aim	

ea	
sea	seam
pea	heap
tea	leap
read	mean
heat	neat
leaf	peak
bean	seat
meat	beat
team	leak
seal	lead

Compound words	
raindrop	sailboat
mainland	railroad
pigtail	

Compound words	
teapot	leapfrog
seaweed	peanut
seaside	seatbelt

Green Level

Phonetically Regular Word Lists

(Group I vowel teams: *oe* and *ie*)

oe	*ie*
toe	pie
doe	tie
foe	die
Joe	lie

Compound words	*Compound words*
tiptoe	magpie
toenail	

Green Level

Phonetically Regular Word Lists

(Group I vowel teams: *ay* and *ow*)

ay	*ow*
may	row
ray	mow
bay	bow
day	bowl
pay	low
hay	own
lay	
way	
say	

Compound words	*Compound words*
Sunday	rowboat

Green Level

Phonetically Regular Word Lists

(Group I vowel teams with blends and digraphs: *ee* and *oa*)

ee			*oa*	
bleed	sleep		boast	roast
cheek	speech		cloak	
creek	speed		coach	
creep	sweep		coast	
green	sweet		croak	
greet	teeth		float	
leech	tree		groan	
sheet	wheel		poach	

Compound words	*Compound words*
beeswax	coastline
freeway	cockroach
sixteen	potroast
speedway	

Green Level

Phonetically Regular Word Lists

(Group I vowel teams with blends and digraphs: *ai*)

ai		
braid	quail	strain
brain	quaint	trail
chain	saint	trait
drain	slain	waist
faint	snail	
faith	Spain	
grain	sprain	
paint	stain	

Compound words	
drainpipe	waistband
paintbox	waistline
paintbrush	

Green Level

Phonetically Regular Word Lists

(Group I vowel teams with blends and digraphs: *ea* and *ay*)

ea	
beach	peach
beast	plead
cheap	reach
clean	speak
cream	sneak
dream	steal
east	teach
feast	treat
	wheat

ay	
clay	spray
gray	stray
play	sway
pray	tray
slay	

Compound words
dreamland
meanwhile
steamboat

Compound words
playmate
playpen

Phonetically Regular Word Lists

(Group I vowel teams with blends and digraphs: *ow*)

ow	
blow	show
crow	slow
flow	snow
flown	stow
glow	throw
grow	

Compound words
showcase
snowflake
snowman

Green Level

Phonetically Regular Word Lists

(inflected -ed endings with no change to base words with Group I vowel teams)

-ed	/d/		/t/
heated	nailed	rained	leaked
needed	aimed	sailed	soaked
waited	failed	sealed	leaped
seated	seemed	peeled	peeked
loaded	moaned	rowed	
	mowed	owned	

Green Level

Phonetically Regular Word Lists

(three-letter blends with closed syllables, final "e," and Group I vowel teams)

str		spr	spl
strip	strain	spring	splat
string	stray	spray	split
stride	street	sprain	splash
stripe	stream		
strike			
stroke			

scr	shr	thr
scrap	shred	throb
scrub	shrub	throne
scrape	shrimp	three
scream	shrine	throw
screen		throat

Road to Reading: A Program for Preventing and Remediating Reading Difficulties by Benita A. Blachman & Darlene M. Tangel

259

Green Level

Phonetically Regular Word Lists

(Group II vowel teams with blends and digraphs: *ou*)

ou	
out	slouch
loud	pound
pout	count
south	found
shout	ground
trout	sound

Multisyllabic words	
outfit	miscount
outside	outhouse
groundhog	counting
greenhouse	southwest

Green Level

Phonetically Regular Word Lists

(Group II vowel teams with blends and digraphs: *oo* as in *sch**oo**l*)

oo		
too	hoop	proof
zoo	food	stool
cool	room	scoot
roof	noon	bloom
pool	coop	droop
mood	zoom	broom
root	booth	smooth

Multisyllabic words	
poolroom	broomstick
schoolroom	noontime
shampoo	poolside
mushroom	toothbrush
rooftop	raccoon
igloo	

Green Level

Phonetically Regular Word Lists

(Group II vowel teams with blends and digraphs: *oo* as in *b**oo**k*)

oo	
book	cook
hood	wool
foot	hook
took	wood
good	shook
brook	stood
woods	

Multisyllabic words	
cookbook	mistook
woodstove	fishhook
schoolbook	footprints

Green Level

Phonetically Regular Word Lists

(Group II vowel teams with blends and digraphs: *ow* and *aw*)

ow	
how	town
cow	drown
now	crowd
bow	clown
howl	brown
owl	crown
down	growl
frown	

aw	
jaw	dawn
law	drawn
raw	hawk
saw	fawn
thaw	flaw
claw	straw
draw	
bawl	

Multisyllabic words
downtown
sundown
countdown

Multisyllabic words
seesaw
jigsaw

Green Level

Phonetically Regular Word Lists

(Group II vowel teams with blends and digraphs: *au* and *oi*)

au	*oi*
haul	oil
Paul	coin
fault	soil
launch	join
	boil
	foil
	spoil
	point
	joint

Multisyllabic words	*Multisyllabic words*
August	tinfoil

Green Level

Phonetically Regular Word Lists

(Group II vowel teams with blends and digraphs: *oy* and *ew*)

oy	*ew*
boy	new
toy	few
joy	stew
Roy	drew
Troy	flew
	blew

Multisyllabic words	*Multisyllabic words*
enjoy	withdrew
annoy	newsprint
cowboy	newsletter
tomboy	newsroom
employ	

Green Level

Phonetically Regular Word Lists

(Group II vowel teams with blends and digraphs: *ea* as in *br__ea__d*)

ea	
head	health
read	breath
bread	spread
meant	thread
sweat	
dealt	
wealth	

Multisyllabic words	
instead	headlight
meadow	headroom
heaven	sweatband
bedspread	breadstick
headband	

Green Level

Phonetically Regular Word Lists

(Group I vowel teams in compound words)

raincoat	teacup
tiptoe	seaweed
peanut	seaside
mailbox	leapfrog
beehive	meantime
coatrack	seatbelt
soapsuds	mailman
raindrop	toenail
mainland	magpie
pigtail	Sunday
sailboat	rowboat
railroad	potpie
teapot	
teammate	

Green Level

Phonetically Regular Word Lists

(two-syllable words with one consonant
between two vowels—VCV)

Divide after the vowel (V/CV)	Divide after the consonant (VC/V)
basic	lem<u>o</u>n[1]
robot	finish
zero	seven
bac<u>o</u>n[1]	robin
silent	planet
motel	cabin
mu<u>s</u>ic[2]	wag<u>o</u>n[1]
tulip	vanish
student	
frozen	

[1]Schwa (the sound of the vowel in an unaccented syllable) often sounds like the short /u/ sound.
[2]/s/ sounds like /z/

 Road to Reading: A Program for Preventing and Remediating Reading Difficulties by Benita A. Blachman & Darlene M. Tangel

Green Level

Sample Sound Board Exercises

(Group I vowel teams)

ee

1. feel – feet – meet – meek – peek – seek – see
2. need – seed – seem – seek – week – weep – jeep
3. seep – seed – weed – feed – feel – reel – eel
4. keen – keep – deep – deed – reed – reel – peel
5. week – meek – meet – beet – bee – see – seen

oa

1. soak – oak – oat – boat – coat – coal – goal
2. toad – load – loan – moan – moat – goat – goal
3. coal – foal – foam – roam – road – load – loaf

ee and oa

1. soap – seep – seek – soak – oak – oat – moat – meet

Green Level

Sample Sound Board Exercises

(Group I vowel teams)

ai

1.   main – pain – pail – mail – maid – aid – ail
2.   aim – ail – sail – bail – bait – wait – wail
3.   laid – raid – rain – rail – fail – pail – pain

ee, oa, and ai

1.   moat – meet – beet – boat – bait – wait – wail
2.   foal – feel – fail – pail – peel – peek – seek – soak
3.   laid – load – road – reed – raid – rail – reel

ea

1.   sea – seal – meal – meat – mean – lean – leap
2.   pea – tea – team – seam – seat – heat – heal
3.   real – read – bead – bean – lean – leaf – leak
4.   weak – leak – peak – pea – sea – seat – neat

Green Level

Sample Sound Board Exercises

(Group I vowel teams)

oe and ie

1. toe – tie – pie – die – doe – foe – hoe
2. lie – die – doe – Joe – woe – toe – tie

ay

1. may – ray – pay – say – bay – lay – day
2. hay – way – day – bay – say – Kay – may

ow

1. tow – low – sow – row – mow – bow – bowl
2. row – low – mow – bow – tow – sow

Green Level

Sample Sound Board Exercises

(Group I vowel teams)

mixed practice

1. raid – rail – real – teal – tea – tow – tie

2. bow – bowl – bail – fail – feel – foal – foe

3. road – read – lead – low – lie – die – doe

4. ail – eel – peel – pail – laid – lie

5. rail – reel – reef – beef – beep – bee – bow – bowl

Green Level

Sample Sound Board Exercises

(Group I vowel teams with blends and digraphs)

ee

1. sleep – sweep – sweet – sleet – greet – green – seen
2. creep – creek – cheek – Greek – greed – speed – bleed

oa

1. got – goat – gloat – float – boat – boast – toast
2. rod – road – roast – coast – coat – coach – roach

ee and oa

1. creek – croak – oak – float – fleet – sleet – sheet

Green Level

Sample Sound Board Exercises

(Group I vowel teams with blends and digraphs)

ai

1. ran – rain – brain – bran – Brad – braid – maid – mad

2. man – main – mail – wail – waist – wait

3. pad – paid – pain – plain – train – trail – snail – sail

4. pan – pain – paint – saint – faint – quaint – quail

ea

1. stem – steam – dream – cream – creak – speak – sneak

2. clean – bean – beach – peach – reach – read – red

3. set – seat – eat – east – beast – best – beat

ay

1. say – stay – sway – way – pay – play – lay

2. ray – tray – gray – clay – play – stay – stray

Green Level

Sample Sound Board Exercises

(Group I vowel teams with blends and digraphs)

ow

1. low – blow – flow – slow – snow – show – shown

2. glow – grow – crow – row – flow – flown – own

mixed practice

1. lay – stay – stow – steep – sleep – slow – low

2. brain – rain – ran – row – crow – bow – blow

3. led – lead – least – lean – loan – load – laid

4. best – beast – boast – roast – rest – test – toast

Green Level

Sample Sound Board Exercises

(Group II vowel teams with blends and digraphs)

ou

1. out – shout – pout – pound – sound – ground

2. cot – count – couch – pouch – pound – found

3. coat – count – cot – couch – slouch – ouch – pouch

*oo (as in sch**oo**l)*

1. food – mood – moon – soon – spoon – spook

2. zoo – zoom – boom – booth – tooth – tool – toolbox*

3. sound – south – spout – spoon – speak – leak – loud - loot

*oo (as in b**oo**k)*

1. book – cook – shook – look

2. stood – steep – creep – creek – crook – croak - count

*Challenge word will need additional letters.

Green Level

Sample Sound Board Exercises

(Group II vowel teams with blends and digraphs)

ow

1. now – how – howl – owl – chow – plow
2. bow – brow – brown – down – town – downtown*
3. grape – green – growl – gray – tray – troop – trout

aw

1. jaw – law – lawn – drawn – draw – saw – seesaw*
2. dawn – fawn – flaw – thaw – straw
3. saw – straw – claw – clown – clean – drown – draw

au

1. haul – Paul – fault – vault
2. Paul – pool – fool –fault – haul – launch – lunch

*Challenge word

Green Level

Sample Sound Board Exercises

(Group II vowel teams with blends and digraphs)

oi

1. oil – soil – coil – coin – join – joint – point
2. oil – boil – spoil – spook – shout – count – coin – point

oy

1. toy – boy – jay – stay – stray – Roy
2. cow – cowboy – boy – Joy – enjoy – employ – Troy

ew

1. few – flew – stew – blew – drew – draw – drawn
2. need – new – drew – dream – cream – crew – crow
3. crew – screw – scream – stream – street – stew – threw

ea

1. head – bread – spread – sprain – rain – read
2. sweat – sweet – meet – meant – mint – sprint

Green Level

Sample Sound Board Exercises

(Group II vowel teams with blends and digraphs)

mixed practice

1. new – now – plow – cow – clown – coin

2. loud – cloud – claw – jaw – joy – soy – saw

3. how – bow – boy – toy – too – tool – stool

4. book – cook – cow – how – howl – owl

5. stew – stout – soil – spoil – speech – sleep – slouch

Sample Reading Sentences

ee

1. I must <u>greet</u> the <u>queen</u>.

2. Did you <u>see</u> Tim last <u>week</u>?

3. A <u>jeep</u> drove up the <u>street</u>.

4. I <u>need</u> to <u>sleep</u>!

5. A <u>bee</u> landed on those <u>sheep</u>.

6. Is the <u>creek</u> <u>deep</u>?

Green Level

Sample Reading Sentences

oa

1. That <u>boat</u> will not <u>float</u>.

2. There is a <u>goat</u> in the <u>road</u>.

3. <u>Joan</u> is a swim <u>coach</u>.

4. The <u>coach</u> helped me make a <u>goal</u>.

5. Did the <u>toad</u> <u>croak</u>* at you?

7. I lost my <u>coat</u>!

*Ask your students if they know the meaning of ***croak***. If not, this is a good opportunity to extend their vocabulary.

Look for other opportunities to extend their vocabulary in each lesson.

Sample Reading Sentences

ai

1. We will ride the <u>train</u>.

2. <u>Gail</u> <u>waits</u> for the <u>mail</u>.

3. I see <u>snail</u> slime on the <u>trail</u>.

4. That is not a <u>raindrop</u>!

5. They will <u>paint</u> the <u>sailboat</u> red.

6. Did it <u>rain</u> and <u>hail</u> last week?

Green Level

Sample Reading Sentences

ea

1. <u>Jean</u> had a bad <u>dream</u>.

2. She will <u>teach</u> us to <u>speak</u> French.

3. That <u>mean</u> dog ate my <u>peach</u>!

4. <u>Please</u> sit in this <u>seat</u>!

5. The <u>seal</u> swam up on the <u>beach</u>.

6. I like to <u>eat</u> ice <u>cream</u>!

Sample Reading Sentences

oe

1. <u>Joe</u> will <u>tiptoe</u> up the path.

2. Did you see the big gray <u>doe</u>?

3. I hit my <u>toe</u> on that rock.

4. I must <u>hoe</u> those seeds.

Sample Reading Sentences

ay

1. Do not drop your lunch <u>tray</u>.

2. What did you <u>say</u>?

3. Did you <u>play</u> with the <u>clay</u>?

4. Please <u>stay</u> until <u>Sunday</u>.

5. I must <u>pay</u> to ride the <u>subway</u>.

6. A <u>gray</u> cat ran that <u>way</u>.

Green Level

Sample Reading Sentences

*ow (as in sn**ow**)*

1. I got a <u>bowl</u> off the shelf.

2. That <u>rowboat</u> is <u>slow</u>.

3. That <u>crow</u> has <u>flown</u> a long way.

4. Did you <u>mow</u> the grass?

5. The pile of <u>snow</u> will <u>grow</u> and <u>grow</u>!

6. I must <u>blow</u> on the hot tea.

Green Level

Sample Reading Sentences

ou

1. The kids will <u>count</u> <u>out</u> <u>loud</u>.

2. I <u>found</u> a dime on the <u>ground</u>.

3. We got a <u>hound</u> at the <u>pound</u>.

4. His <u>shout</u> is quite <u>loud</u>.

5. Are there <u>clouds</u> at the <u>South</u> Pole?

6. I ate a <u>pound</u> of <u>trout</u> at lunch.

Green Level

Sample Reading Sentences

*oo (as in sch**oo**l)*

1.   This <u>room</u> feels <u>too</u> <u>cool</u>.

2.   The <u>bloom</u> will <u>droop</u> in the sun.

3.   <u>Shoot</u> the ball into the <u>hoop</u>!

4.   I need to <u>cool</u> off in the <u>pool</u>.

5.   We will go to the <u>zoo</u> at <u>noon</u>.

6.   He spilled <u>food</u> in the <u>booth</u>.

Sample Reading Sentences

*oo (as in b**oo**k)*

1. I <u>stood</u> in the <u>brook</u>.

2. He <u>took</u> the <u>wood</u> into the shed.

3. This was a very <u>good</u> <u>book</u>!

4. I <u>shook</u> the bug off my <u>foot</u>.

5. Did you get a <u>look</u> at the <u>crook</u>?

6. I lost my <u>good</u> <u>wool</u> coat!

Green Level

Sample Reading Sentences

*ow (as in pl**ow**)*

1. How can I get <u>down</u> from this tree?

2. The <u>clown</u> made the <u>crowd</u> smile.

3. Can we go to <u>town</u> <u>now</u>?

4. I see a <u>brown</u> <u>owl</u> on that branch.

5. My dog likes to <u>howl</u> and <u>growl</u>.

6. Please do not <u>frown</u> and <u>scowl</u>!*

*Do your students know the meaning of **scowl**?

If not, this is another opportunity to extend vocabulary.

Green Level

Sample Reading Sentences

aw

1. Did you see the <u>claw</u> on that <u>hawk</u>?

2. I saw the ice <u>thaw</u> at <u>dawn</u>.

3. The cow had <u>straw</u> in his <u>jaws</u>.

4. He can <u>draw</u> a <u>crawfish</u>.*

5. I do not like to eat <u>raw</u> fish!

6. The dog likes to <u>sprawl</u>* on the <u>lawn</u>.

*Do your students know the meanings of **crawfish** or **sprawl**?

Sample Reading Sentences

au

1. <u>Paul</u> needs to <u>haul</u> that pile of wood.

2. The cash is safe inside the <u>vault</u>.*

3. It was my <u>fault</u> that we got lost.

4. They will <u>launch</u>* the rocket in <u>August</u>.

5. I will <u>haul</u> those rocks up the hill.

*Do your students know the meanings of **vault** or **launch**?

Green Level

Sample Reading Sentences

oi

1. We must <u>boil</u> the eggs or they will <u>spoil</u>.

2. The <u>soil</u> must be <u>moist</u> so the plant can grow.

3. I plan to <u>join</u> that club.

4. Will you <u>point</u> to the <u>oil</u> can?

5. I found a <u>coin</u> in the <u>soil</u>.

Green Level

Sample Reading Sentences

oy

1. The <u>boy</u> broke his <u>toy</u>.

2. I do not like <u>soy</u> milk.

3. I feel <u>joy</u> when I see my pal <u>Roy</u>!

4. <u>Troy</u> will let me play with his <u>toy</u>.

Green Level

Sample Reading Sentences

ew

1. The wind <u>blew</u> my <u>new</u> kite.

2. We <u>flew</u> home on a plane.

3. There are a <u>few</u> <u>new</u> kids in the class.

4. The <u>crew</u> did not like the meat <u>stew</u>.

5. I <u>drew</u> a cat for my mom.

6. The plant <u>grew</u> big in the sun.

Green Level

Sample Reading Sentences

*ea (as in br**ea**d)*

1. I hit my <u>head</u> on the side of the bed.

2. Do you like this homemade <u>bread</u>?

3. The tire <u>tread</u> fell off the wheel.

4. Use the black <u>thread</u> to mend those pants.

5. The hot sun made us <u>sweat</u>.

6. That <u>bread</u> is good for your <u>health</u>.

Sample Dictation Exercises

(Group I vowel teams)

ee

e   **ee**
set   meet
bed   feed
      deep

I will feed the eel.

ee   **e**
see   met
peel   fed
deep

I need to keep the jeep.

e   **ee**
led   reed
red   need
      peel

Meet me this week.

Green Level

Sample Dictation Exercises

(Group I vowel teams)

oa

o	**oa**
pop	soap
sob	goat
	coal

The toad sat on the road.

ee	**oa**
weep	loaf
seek	soak
	goal

The goat has a coat.

oa	**ee**
boat	bee
oak	seen
moan	

The boat is made of oak.

Green Level

Sample Dictation Exercises

(Group I vowel teams)

ai

_a_	**_ai_**
mad	pain
sap	maid
	wait

The rain fell.

_oa_	**_ai_**
load	main
goal	laid
	tail

Jen has a pail of bait.

_ee_	**_oa_**	**_ai_**
beet	boat	bait
reed		raid

I paid for the sail.

Green Level

Sample Dictation Exercises

(Group I vowel teams)

ea

<table>
<tr><td><u>e</u></td><td><u>ea</u></td></tr>
<tr><td>led</td><td>bead</td></tr>
<tr><td>beg</td><td>seat</td></tr>
<tr><td></td><td>heap</td></tr>
</table>

I will eat the beans.

<table>
<tr><td><u>oa</u></td><td><u>ai</u></td><td><u>ea</u></td></tr>
<tr><td>road</td><td>raid</td><td>read</td></tr>
<tr><td>loaf</td><td></td><td>leaf</td></tr>
</table>

That seal is neat!

<table>
<tr><td><u>o-e</u></td><td><u>ai</u></td><td><u>ea</u></td></tr>
<tr><td>rode</td><td>raid</td><td>lead</td></tr>
<tr><td>tone</td><td>tail</td><td>seam</td></tr>
</table>

My team will beat them.

Green Level

Sample Dictation Exercises

(Group I vowel teams)

oe

o   **oe**
job   Joe
chop   doe
          foe

I will stub my toe.

---

ea   **ai**   **oe**
meat   sail   toe
bean   doe

Joe has a hoe.

---

ee   **ai**   **oe**
beep   nail   Joe
weed   aim

The doe ran fast.

Road to Reading: A Program for Preventing and Remediating Reading Difficulties by Benita A. Blachman & Darlene M. Tangel

Green Level

Sample Dictation Exercises

(Group I vowel teams)

ie

i	*ie*
pick	tie
wig	pie
	lie

I will not let my fish die.

ie	*ai*	*ea*
lie	raid	read
die		leaf

I will get that pie.

ai	*ea*	*ie*
pain	mean	pie
maid	beak	

I ate pie.

Green Level

Sample Dictation Exercises

(Group I vowel teams)

ay

a	*ay*
bad	say
flap	may
	way

I must pay Bob.

ee	*ie*	*ay*
seen	tie	ray
feel		hay

I see a ray of sun.

ay	*ai*
lay	pain
day	fail
	wait

I will lay on the rug.

Green Level

Sample Dictation Exercises

(Group I vowel teams)

*ow (as in sn**ow**)*

ay	**ow**
pay	mow
say	tow
	bow

I can bowl.

ea	**ai**	**ow**
sea	wail	tow
real		low

The tow truck is red.

ay	**ai**	**ow**
may	bait	bowl
	sail	low

I will mow the grass.

Road to Reading: A Program for Preventing and Remediating Reading Difficulties by Benita A. Blachman & Darlene M. Tangel

Sample Dictation Exercises

(Group I vowel teams with blends and digraphs)

ee

e	**ee**
best	sleet
red	sweet
	teeth

Pat went to sleep.

ee	**i-e**
cheek	wipe
creek	smile
speech	

The green tree is big.

a-e	**i-e**	**ee**
same	shine	cheek
grade		feel

Sweep up this mess.

Green Level

Sample Dictation Exercises

(Group I vowel teams with blends and digraphs)

oa

o	**oa**
stop	boat
shop	roast
	groan

The tube will float.

ee	**oa**
speed	oat
meet	coach
	float

I ate the toast.

oa	**ee**
boat	tree
throat	sheet
goal	

The green frog croaks.

Green Level

Sample Dictation Exercises

(Group I vowel teams with blends and digraphs)

ai

a	*ai*
fast	trail
grab	rain
	waist

I will paint the stain.

oa	*ai*
float	mail
road	plain
	braid

A snail sat in the path.

ee	*oa*	*ai*
sheep	boast	faint
bleed		brain

Dave will hike the trail.

Green Level

Sample Dictation Exercises

(Group I vowel teams with blends and digraphs)

ea

e	**ea**
sled	dream
best	speak
	cheap

I will eat a treat.

i-e	**ai**	**ea**
lime	train	sneak
prize		beast

Clean up this trash.

ea	**ai**	**a-e**
wheat	claim	shape
east	chain	

Sam will teach us to swim.

Green Level

Sample Dictation Exercises

(Group I vowel teams with blends and digraphs)

ay

<table>
<tr><td><u>**a**</u></td><td><u>**ay**</u></td></tr>
<tr><td>glad</td><td>ray</td></tr>
<tr><td>sad</td><td>sway</td></tr>
<tr><td></td><td>gray</td></tr>
</table>

Tim plays a fun game.

<table>
<tr><td><u>**ea**</u></td><td><u>***i***</u></td><td><u>**ay**</u></td></tr>
<tr><td>cream</td><td>slip</td><td>clay</td></tr>
<tr><td>feast</td><td></td><td>stay</td></tr>
</table>

That cat is gray.

Green Level

Sample Dictation Exercises

(Group I vowel teams with blends and digraphs)

ow (as in sn**ow**)

_ay_	**_ow_**
play	low
way	slow
	crow

The snow is deep.

_ea_	**_ai_**	**_ow_**
speak	snail	flow
treat		throw

The wind will blow.

Green Level

Sample Dictation Exercises

(Group II vowel teams with blends and digraphs)

ou

ou	**oe**
out	doe
loud	toe
count	

I found a dime on the ground.

o	**ou**	**oa**
bock	shout	boat
spot	sound	float

The kids will count out loud.

Green Level

Sample Dictation Exercises

(Group II vowel teams with blends and digraphs)

*oo (as in sch**oo**l)*

oo	**o-e**	**ai**
pool	rode	paint
food	bone	
zoom		

The bloom will droop in the sun.

o	**oo**	**ou**
clock	smooth	couch
	roof	pout
	tooth	

We went to the zoo at noon.

Green Level

Sample Dictation Exercises

(Group II vowel teams with blends and digraphs)

*oo (as in b**oo**k)*

oo	**ow**
wood	flow
stood	grown
cook	

I took the book home.

ou	**oo**	**o**
trout	hook	box
cloud	brook	drop

He shook the mud off his foot.

Green Level

Sample Dictation Exercises

(Group II vowel teams with blends and digraphs)

*ow (as in pl**ow**)*

ow	**o**	**ee**
now	stop	teeth
howl		sleep
crowd		

I see a brown owl.

ow	**oo**	**ay**
cow	tool	stay
down	mood	
plow		

The clown went to town.

Green Level

Sample Dictation Exercises

(Group II vowel teams with blends and digraphs)

aw

_aw_	**_a_**	**_oo_**
law	fast	foot
thaw		good
straw		

I saw a fawn in the woods.

_ow_	**_aw_**	**_a_**
how	drawn	strap
frown	jaw	
gown		

The hawk had a big claw.

Green Level

Sample Dictation Exercises

(Group II vowel teams with blends and digraphs)

au

au	*a*	*ea*
haul	land	team
fault	glad	clean

Paul will haul the bucket.

oi

oi	*aw*
point	draw
boil	raw
join	

I found a coin in the soil.

oi	*oo*	*i*
coin	smooth	grip
soil	broom	stick

Did you join the club?

Green Level

Sample Dictation Exercise

(Group II vowel teams with blends and digraphs)

oy

oy	**o-e**	**o**
joy	throne	clock
Roy	broke	
boy		

The boy got a toy to enjoy.

ew

ew	**aw**	**e**
few	claw	fresh
stew	shawl	
drew		

The boy flew a new kite.

ea

ee	**ea**	**a-e**
sweep	head	scrape
speech	wealth	blame

Spread grape jam on the bread.

Blue Level

Goals for the Blue Level

When the students complete this level, they should be able to do the following:

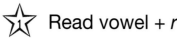 Read vowel + *r* words (e.g., c*ar*, h*orn*, b*ird*, t*urn*, f*ern*).

Read selected words with the suffix *-ly* (e.g., slow**ly**) and inflected ending *-es* (e.g., teach**es**)

Read words with *-ink*, *-ank*, and *-unk* (e.g., p**ink**, b**ank**, tr**unk**).

Read words with the *-all* and *-alk* patterns (e.g., b**all**, t**alk**).

Read multisyllabic words made up of previously learned syllable patterns (e.g., *yardstick, pineapple, fantastic, misunderstood*).

Step 1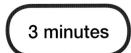

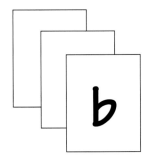

Review Sound–Symbol Correspondences

Materials

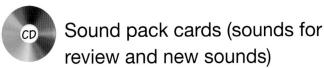

Sound pack cards (sounds for review and new sounds)

Procedures

Use your sound pack of previously learned letters to continue to review selected consonant digraphs, short and long vowels, and vowel teams with your students.

Remember, the goal is to develop fluency, not boredom.

Vowel + r

Vowel + r combinations should be written in red and added to the sound pack as they are taught. The students should learn the sounds /ar/ as in **c_ar_**, /or/ as in **c_or_n**, /ir/ as in **b_ir_d**, /ur/ as in **t_ur_n**, and /er/ as in **f_er_n**.

> The students may encounter words in which *or* makes an /er/ sound (instead of /or/ as in **c_or_n**). For example, *or* makes an /er/ sound in **w_or_m, w_or_d**, and *doct_or_.* When the students see these words, just tell them that these words are a "special case." If needed, read the words for the students.

Step 2

Teach or Review New Decoding Skill

5–7 minutes

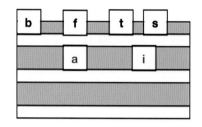

Materials

 Sound board for each student

 Consonant letters and digraphs in the top pocket (only include those needed to make words for a particular lesson)

 Vowel letters and vowel teams in the middle pocket (only include those needed to make words for a particular lesson)

Procedures

Use the sound board to introduce words with vowel + *r*. Each vowel + *r* combination *(ar, ir, or, er,* and *ur)* should be written in red (e.g., ar) on a single card.

Introduce each combination by selecting sound board exercises from the lists below. Some lists require changing more than one sound as new words are made.

ar

car ----→ card ----→ hard ----→ yard ----→ yarn ----→ barn

bark ----→ stark ----→ dark ----→ shark ----→ sharp ----→ harp

card ----→ cart ----→ start ----→ smart ----→ far ----→ farm

march ----→ chart ----→ charm ----→ arm ----→ farm ----→ harm

or

horn ----→ thorn ----→ corn ----→ cork ----→ stork ----→ storm

corn ----→ born ----→ short ----→ stork ----→ pork ----→ fork ----→ torch

er

her ----→ herd ----→ fern ----→ stern ----→ perk ----→ perch

ir

bird ----→ third ----→ thirst ----→ first ----→ skirt ----→ dirt

skirt ----→ shirt ----→ thirst ----→ third ----→ first ----→ fir

Step
2

ur

blur ----▶ blurt ----▶ hurt ----▶ hurl ----▶ curl ----▶ curb

burn ----▶ turn ----▶ turf ----▶ surf ----▶ slurp* ----▶ burp ----▶ burst

*Do the students know what it means to **slurp**?

mixed practice

hard ----▶ card ----▶ cord ----▶ bird ----▶ third ----▶ thorn

star ----▶ start ----▶ stork ----▶ torch ----▶ sport ----▶ port

dart ----▶ dirt ----▶ shirt ----▶ short ----▶ shark ----▶ park

far ----▶ for ----▶ fir ----▶ first ----▶ firm ----▶ form ----▶ farm

arm ----▶ farm ----▶ barn ----▶ born ----▶ burn ----▶ burnt

born ----▶ burn ----▶ burp ----▶ curb ----▶ cart ----▶ short

charm ----▶ harm ----▶ harp ----▶ sharp ----▶ shirt ----▶ flirt

churn ----▶ church ----▶ porch ----▶ pork ----▶ park ----▶ stark

Remember to look for opportunities to extend vocabulary in each lesson.

See the Additional Materials section at the end of this level for lists of one-syllable words, as well as lists of multisyllable words with the vowel + *r* pattern.

Step 3

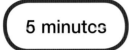

5 minutes

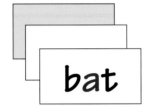

bat

Review Phonetically Regular Words (PRWs) and High Frequency Words (HFWs)

Materials

 Phonetically regular word (PRW) cards (only those words you plan to use in a particular lesson)

 High frequency word (HFW) cards (only those words that you plan to use in a particular lesson)

One dry erase board, one dry erase marker, and one eraser for the teacher

Step
3

Procedures

The goal of this activity is to develop fluency. The focus is on the phonetically regular words, with a few high frequency words included.

You may want to increase the number of words you have in your word card pack. Remember, however, that this step should take no more than 5 minutes and preferably less time as the students' word reading skills become more fluent. Continue to focus on the phonetically regular words, with a few high frequency words included each day.

The phonetically regular words (PRWs) should consist of words with the new patterns you are teaching (vowel + *r*).

In addition, the following types of words will be introduced in this step on the dry erase board:

- Suffix *-ly* (e.g., *slowly*) and ending *-es* (e.g., *teaches*)

- "Special case" words (e.g., *-ink* as in *pink*, *-ank* as in *bank*, *-unk* as in *trunk*)

- Special case words (e.g., *-all* as in *ball*, *-alk* as in *talk*)

Words with previously learned syllable patterns (e.g., closed and open syllables, final "e" syllables, vowel teams) should also be included in your phonetically regular word (PRW) cards and reviewed.

Remember that the phonetically regular words (PRWs) and high frequency words (HFWs) should be written on different colored cards.

Step

3

Phonetically Regular Words (PRWs)

Vowel + r Words

- Once the students can successfully make vowel + r words with ar (e.g., c**ar**, ch**ar**t) on the sound board, you can add words with ar to your phonetically regular word (PRW) cards and introduce words with or (e.g., c**or**n, sp**or**t) on the sound board.

- Follow the same procedure with words with or (e.g., c**or**n), er (e.g., h**er**), ir (e.g., b**ir**d), and ur (e.g., b**ur**n), adding words with these patterns to the phonetically regular word (PRW) cards as soon as students can make those words on the sound board.

A starter set of PRWs has been provided below. The Additional Materials section at the end of this level contains more lists of vowel + r words. Remember to write the vowel + r combination in red.

Starter Set of Blue Level Phonetically Regular Word (PRW) Cards

Vowel + r

ar	or	ir	ur	er
card	corn	bird	curl	her
hard	torn	dirt	burn	jerk
part	fort	sir	burp	fern
bark	form	firm	turf	verb
scar	born		surf	perk*
star	pork		hurl	
dart	sort		hurt	
car	worn		fur	
far	cork		turn	
jar			blur*	

*Do the students know the meanings of **blur** and **perk**?

327

Words with the Suffix -ly and Inflected Ending -es

It is a good idea to introduce words with the suffix -ly (e.g., slow**ly**) and the inflected ending -es (e.g., teach**es**) in this step of the lesson.

> **Please note:** The dry erase board will be used to introduce the new concepts on the following pages.

Adding the Suffix -ly

To introduce -ly, write the following on the dry erase board:

> **slow + ly = slowly**

- Tell the students the sound that the -ly makes and read the word.

- Write the words in the list below on the dry erase board.

- Ask one student to read the base word. Give that student the dry erase maker and have him or her add an -ly to the word and then read the new word.

- hard + ly = hardly
- quick + ly = quickly
- week + ly = weekly
- swift + ly = swiftly

- safe + ly = safely
- night + ly = nightly
- bright + ly = brightly
- tight + ly = tightly

> **Please note:** When the suffix -ly is added to the word, it adds meaning. The new word tells how, when, or to what degree.

Step 3

Adding -es to Nouns and Verbs

In the Orange Level, students learned to make plurals by adding *-s* to words when there was no change to the base word. In this level, the students learn to make plurals to words requiring an *-es*.

To introduce *-es*, write the following on the dry erase board:

box + es = boxes

- Tell the students that some words that name a person, place, or thing (nouns) require an *-es* to make the word mean more than one (i.e., to make it plural).

- Read the word *boxes* for the students.

- Next, write the list of words below and have the students read each word.

dishes

brushes

churches

beaches

Students will also be reading action words (verbs) that require the -es ending. Have the students read the following words:

> **teaches**
>
> **mixes**
>
> **fixes**
>
> **buzzes**

To provide additional reinforcement, read each sentence and ask the students to tell you which word from the previous list best completes the sentence:

1.   Mrs. Jones _____ the children how to read.

2.   Dad _____the paint.

3.   Jane _____the car.

4.   The bee _____in the yard.

> ***Please note:*** Any word (noun or verb) that ends in *-sh*, *-ch*, *-x*, *-s,* or *-z* requires the addition of *-es* to the noun or verb form. A good way to help students remember this is by having them think about placing each of these endings on their toes or fingers.
>
> -s
> -x
> -z
> -ch
> -sh

Include words with the *-ly* and *-es* endings in your phonetically regular word (PRW) cards.

Words with -ink, -ank, or -unk (a Special Case)

It is a good idea to introduce words with *-ink, -ank,* and *-unk* patterns in this step of the lesson.

> Although the *-nk* ending blend was introduced in the Orange Level, words that end in *-ank* (e.g., b**ank**, th**ank**) were not included previously because the letter *a* takes on the long /a/ sound. Even though words that end in *-ink* (e.g., p**ink**, th**ink**) were included earlier, these, too, are a special case because the letter *i* takes on the long /e/ sound. Words ending in *-unk* (e.g., b**unk**, tr**unk**), however, retain the short /u/ sound. This pattern is included here because *-ink, -ank,* and *-unk* are often grouped for instruction.

- Put each of the following lists of words on the dry erase board, writing and reading one list at a time.

-ink	**-ank**	**-unk**
ink	sank	bunk
wink	bank	trunk
sink	tank	skunk
mink	thank	junk
drink	crank	dunk
pink	drank	flunk
think	spank	shrunk

- Underline the special pattern in each list.

- Read the first word for the students; then, have the students read the remaining words on the list.

Include words with the *-ink, -ank,* and *-unk* patterns in your PRW cards.

Words with -all and -alk (a Special Case)

It is a good idea to introduce the -all and -alk patterns on the dry erase board during this step.

- To introduce -all, write the following words on the dry erase board:

all

b**all**

t**all**

f**all**

c**all**

h**all**

st**all**

sm**all**

- As shown, underline -all in each word and tell the students that it says /all/ as in b**all**.

- Have the students read the rest of the words.

- To make this exercise more challenging, you can add compound words to the list.

> **ballgame**
> **football**
> **basketball**
> **baseball**
> **snowball**

- Next, introduce *-alk* by writing the following words on the dry erase board:

> t<u>alk</u>
> w<u>alk</u>
> ch<u>alk</u>
> st<u>alk</u>

- As shown, underline *-alk* in each word and tell the students that it says /alk/ as in *talk*.

- Have the students read the rest of the words.

- To make this exercise more challenging, you can add two-syllable and compound words to the list:

> **sidewalk**
> **beanstalk**
> **walkway**
> **walkman**

Compound Words

Continue to introduce compound words made up of the syllable types the students have already learned.

For example, some of the new compound words that you may want to introduce at this level include the following:

birdbath	shortcake
shortcut	forgave
northwest	yardstick
blackbird	forget
barnyard	newspaper
zookeeper	porkchop

For some groups, you may want to continue to introduce the compound words by putting the individual words that make up each compound word (e.g., *black, bird*) on separate cards.

Step 3

- Read the individual words first.

- Next, physically move the cards together to show the students how compound words are made up of words they already know how to read.

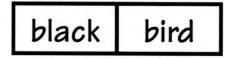

See the Additional Materials section at the end of this level for other compound words that include the new vowel + *r* syllable pattern.

Remember to review the Additional Materials sections in previous levels of the program for compound words that are made up of the syllable types the students have already learned.

Compound words can be put on white index cards for review, just as you would with any other phonetically regular words in this step.

In addition to compound words, many students will now be able to read complex multisyllabic words made up of previously learned syllable patterns (e.g., *fantastic, misunderstood*).

> ***Please note:*** The Blue Level Additional Materials section includes two- and three-syllable words that contain the new vowel + *r* pattern (e.g., *h<u>or</u>net, hib<u>er</u>nate*).

High Frequency Words (HFWs) 201–250

The following high frequency words (HFWs) from Fry and Kress (2006) can be taught and added to your word card pack. You might want to pretest the students on these HFWs at this level and create an individualized list of HFWs that the students still need to learn. A High Frequency Word Assessment form for the Blue Level and individual word cards are included on the CD-ROM.

*high	every	near	*add	*food	*between	*own
*below	country	*plant	*last	*school	father	*keep
*tree	**never	**start	city	earth	eye	*light
thought	*head	**under	story	*saw	*left	don't
*few	*while	along	**might	close	something	*seem
*next	**hard	*open	example	*begin	*life	always
*those	both	**paper	together	*got	group	often
*run						

Adapted from *The Reading Teacher's Book of Lists, Fifth Edition,* by E.B. Fry and J. Kress
© 2006 Jossey-Bass. Reprinted with permission from John Wiley & Sons, Inc.

*Students learned to decode words written in red, orange, yellow, and green during the Red, Orange, Yellow, and Green levels in this program, respectively.

**Students will be learning to decode the words written in blue at this level in the program.

Step 3

Once each high frequency word has been mastered by most of the students, you might want to file the word in the back of a high frequency word box in alphabetical order. These words should be reviewed on a regular basis in Step 3 of your lesson to make sure that the students remember them.

As is evident from the many high frequency words (HFWs) in the Blue Level that appear color-coded in the chart on the previous page, students who have learned the five syllable types presented thus far can use their decoding skill to read over 60% of the high frequency words included in this level. This greatly reduces the number of high frequency words that might otherwise need to be memorized.

An Important Note About Developing Fluency

Remember, the overall goal of this activity is to develop fluency at the word level. A hallmark of good readers is the ability to read both accurately and fluently.

Step
3

To help students develop fluency, you will need to have the students read the words more than once.

Activities for Developing Fluency

- When the students read the words for the second time, try using an hourglass to encourage the students to move more quickly. The students like to see how many words they can read before the sand runs out.

- Use a stopwatch with the group and have the students see how long it takes to read all the words in the card pack for that day.

- Students can also use the hourglass or stopwatch while working in pairs. Each student tries to read his or her words more quickly than during his or her previous reading. This way, the students are encouraged to improve their own times and not compete with each other.

Step 4

Read Orally in Context

Materials

Selected decodable readers (see Blue Level chart)

Selected books/stories from your classroom or school library or basal program (suggested book titles appear in Appendix B)

Procedures

In this section we list a variety of options for reading material. The choices you make will depend on the skill level of your students.

At this level, students should be able to read a wide variety of texts, including chapter books, nonfiction, poetry, and plays, with corrective feedback to develop fluency.

As noted in the *Report of the National Reading Panel* (National Institute of Child Heath and Human Development, 2000), "Fluent readers are able to read orally with speed, accuracy, and proper expression. Fluency is one of several critical factors for reading comprehension" (p. 11).

Step
4

Decodable Book Chart for the Blue Level

To help you select books for your groups, we have created decodable book charts for the first five levels of this program.

Books on this chart are arranged by the vowel + *r* syllable pattern being taught in this level.

This chart is meant to help you individualize instruction for your students. ***Remember, other decodable books may be substituted for those on the chart.***

There will be a great deal of variation in the number of decodable books that each student needs to read. Some students may continue to need to read decodable readers, such as those on the chart, to reinforce the patterns they are learning and to become accurate and fluent. Other students at this level may no longer need decodable readers. These students will be much more independent and will be able to read a much wider variety of carefully selected materials, such as chapter books, nonfiction, poetry, and plays.

Step

4

Blue Level Decodable Book Chart

PP = Primary Phonics

		Title	Vowel + *r*	New Words*
\multicolumn{5}{c}{**Decodable Books with Vowel + *r***}				
1	PP 4-6	*The Go-Cart*	*ar*	*cardboard*
2	PP 4-7	*The Lost Horse*	*ar, or*	*afraid, before, stepped*
3	PP 4-8	*The Brave Hunter*	*ar, er*	*care, scare, chair*
4	PP 4-10	*The Hard Worker*	*ar, or, er*	*calendar, labor, blizzard, flavor*
5	PP 4-9	*The Birdfeeder*	*or, ir, ur, er*	*Sue*

*The *New Words* category in the decodable book chart includes both high frequency words that have not been taught yet in this program and phonetically regular words with patterns that have not been taught yet.

An Important Note About Building Fluency

Although many of your students will be becoming more fluent as they progress through the levels of the program, others will still require opportunities for ***frequent repeated readings*** of text with corrective feedback to build fluency.

As in the Orange Level and Green Level, in addition to reading texts, we have also provided ***Sample Reading Sentences*** in the Additional Materials section at the end of this level for further practice of words with vowel + *r*. Review previous suggestions in the Orange Level for ways to use these sentences.

Feel free to shorten the sentences and/or substitute words with simpler constructions for any of the words we have included.

Additional opportunities for repeated reading can occur by putting completed books in a center where students can reread them at other times during the day. This should not, however, replace repeated reading with corrective feedback by the teacher because repeated reading with corrective feedback has been found to be the most effective method for developing fluency.

An Important Note About Selecting Books

Students at this level should have opportunities to read from a wide variety of texts.

Most students may be proficient enough to read the text in carefully selected trade books, such as chapter books, nonfiction, poetry, and plays. Other students may continue to need more support from the teacher (e.g., needing the teacher to supply unknown words or alternating reading when texts become longer, as in chapter books).

Appendix B contains some titles of trade books that many students at this level will be able to read successfully. ***Again, feel free to substitute your favorite books for students reading at this level.***

Step 5 Dictation

5–7 minutes

Materials

Dictation notebook for each student

Pencil

One dry erase board, one dry erase marker, and one eraser for the teacher

Procedures

- Each dictation exercise should include five or six words and one short sentence that uses words with the same phonetic pattern.

- At the beginning of each notebook dictation session, ask the students to put the date on the top of that day's page.

- Tell the students which vowels they will be using for that day's lesson. These vowels will be their column headings.

- Have the students write the vowel headings on their page to help organize the dictation.

Once the students have set up the paper for the day's dictation, review the sounds of the vowels in the vowel headings before dictating the first word.

Step
5

- Have the students write each word under the appropriate vowel as the word is dictated.

- The sound pack vowel cards from Step 1 corresponding to the vowels that you are using in dictation can be placed on the table as a reference for the students.

- Continue to review words with short and long vowels with blends and digraphs. You should also review vowel team words using headings.

Once students can successfully make words with vowel + *r* (beginning with *ar* as in *car* and *chart*) on the sound board and you have included that pattern in other steps of the lesson, you are ready to include words with that pattern in dictation.

As students learn additional vowel + *r* combinations (*or, ir, er, ur*), include words with these patterns in dictation.

> ***Please note:*** The patterns *ir, er,* and *ur* all have the same sound—the /er/ as in ***bird***. Therefore, words with these patterns should not be included in the same dictation lesson.

Examples of notebook dictation pages: Vowel team review

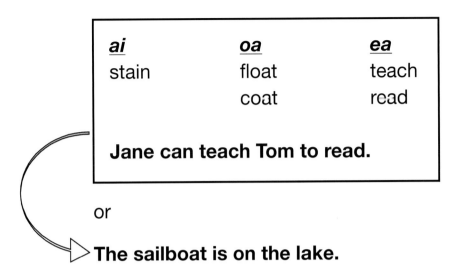

ai	*oa*	*ea*
stain	float	teach
	coat	read

Jane can teach Tom to read.

or

The sailboat is on the lake.

Examples of notebook dictation pages: Vowel + *r*

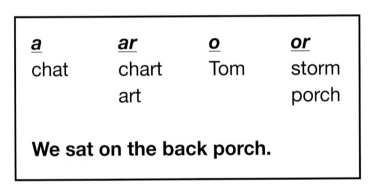

a	*ar*	*o*	*or*
chat	chart	Tom	storm
	art		porch

We sat on the back porch.

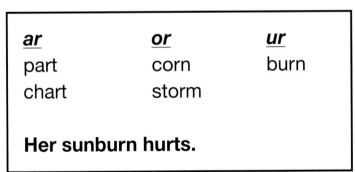

ar	*or*	*ur*
part	corn	burn
chart	storm	

Her sunburn hurts.

Refer to the Additional Materials section at the end of this level for more sample dictation exercises for words with vowel + *r.*

If you are working with more advanced students and would like more challenging sentences for dictation, try using some of the Blue Level Sample Reading Sentences.

You can also vary the format when using these sentences by sending one student to the board to write the dictated sentence and asking the other students to provide corrective feedback, if necessary. You can also use the dry erase board and select one student to write the dictated sentence. After critiquing the sentence, you or the student can select the next student to use the dry erase board to write the next dictated sentence.

Additional Materials

Blue Level

Phonetically Regular Word Lists (*ar* and *or*)

ar			*or*	
car	Mark	start	corn	horn
part	yard	chart	sort	porch
art	cart	smart	pork	thorn
park	harm	spark	cord	sport
arm	dart	shark	fort	short
jar	bark	March	born	storm
Carl	star	scarf	form	north
dark	farm	charm	torn	stork
far	yarn	sharp	fork	torch
card	harp	scar	cork	snort
hard	barn		worn	

Blue Level

Phonetically Regular Word Lists (*ir*, *ur*, and *er*)

ir		*ur*	*er*
sir	squirt	turn	her
fir	swirl	burn	fern
bird	squirm	curb	Bert
dirt		fur	stern
firm		curl	herd
shirt		hurt	verb
third		surf	perch
chirp		blur	perk
first		slurp	jerk
birth		burst	clerk
thirst		church	
skirt		burnt	
twirl		blurt	

Blue Level

Phonetically Regular Word Lists

(two-syllable words and compound words)

ar	
carpet	sharpen
target	darkness
garden	barber
market	harvest
partner	garlic
barnyard	yardstick

or	
hornet	order
northern	corner
morning	perform
forget	shortstop
forgave	forbid
northwest	shortcut

ir
birthday
squirrel
thirteen
birdbath

ur
further
disturb
surprise
purple
Thursday

er	
enter	lantern
termite	desert
perfume	hermit
perfect	Albert
never	river
silver	winter

Blue Level

Phonetically Regular Word Lists

(three-syllable words)

ar	*or*	*er*
department	tornado	remember
argument	porcupine	hibernate*
		understand
		butterfly

*Do the students know what it means to **hibernate**?

If not, this is a good opportunity to expand vocabulary.

Blue Level

Sample Reading Sentences

ar

1. It is not <u>smart</u> to swim with a <u>shark</u>!

2. We will <u>start</u> the <u>car</u> and drive to the <u>park</u>.

3. The <u>farm</u> has a <u>barn</u> and a big <u>yard</u>.

4. You can see the <u>stars</u> when it gets <u>dark</u>.

5. That <u>sharp</u> cut made a <u>scar</u> on my <u>arm</u>.

6. <u>Mark</u> gave <u>part</u> of his lunch to <u>Clark</u>.

7. We can make a <u>scarf</u> with that <u>yarn</u>.

or

1. The <u>torch</u> lit the path in the <u>storm</u>.

2. Use your <u>fork</u> to eat your <u>corn</u>.

3. What <u>sort</u> of <u>sports</u> do you like to play?

4. I was <u>born</u> in New York.

5. The pants were <u>torn</u> and <u>worn</u> out.

6. The <u>storm</u> blew in from the <u>north</u>.

7. Please <u>form</u> a <u>short</u> line at the <u>door</u>.

Blue Level

Sample Reading Sentences

ir

1. The <u>bird</u> flew to the <u>fir</u> tree.

2. The <u>girl</u> will <u>twirl</u> her <u>skirt</u>.

3. Your <u>shirt</u> has <u>dirt</u> on it.

4. I won <u>first</u> place in the race.

5. Did the <u>bird</u> in the <u>birch</u> tree <u>chirp</u>?

6. He is in the <u>third</u> grade.

7. I will <u>stir</u> the mix for the <u>birthday</u> cake.

Blue Level

Sample Reading Sentences

ur

1. My cat will <u>curl</u> up and lick her <u>fur</u>.

2. My hand <u>hurt</u> from the <u>burn</u>.

3. The tire <u>burst</u> when it hit the <u>curb</u>.

4. Do you like to <u>surf</u>?

5. <u>Turn</u> left on the street next to the <u>church</u>.

6. Do not <u>slurp</u> the milk.

7. The boy ran so fast that he was a <u>blur</u>.

er

1. The <u>clerk</u> gave him cash after the sale.

2. Get that <u>herd</u>* of cows off the road!

3. I gave her a <u>stern</u>* look.

4. I will <u>perch</u>* on the <u>stern</u>* of the ship.

*Ask your students if they know the multiple meanings of **herd**, **stern**, and **perch**.

If not, this is a good opportunity to expand vocabulary.

Look for other opportunities to extend vocabulary in each lesson.

Blue Level

Sample Dictation Exercises

ar

_a_	**_ar_**
grab	shark
last	arm
	march

Mark is in the yard.

_ar_	**_a-e_**
sharp	made
smart	name
cart	

The park is dark.

_ar_	**_ow_**
art	snow
jar	bowl
far	

Tar got on the car.

Blue Level

Sample Dictation Exercises

or

_or_   **o**
short   hot
north   lock
porch

I ate corn with my fork.

_ar_   **_or_**
star   torn
barn   sort
         storm

A bad storm hit the barn.

_ay_   **_or_**   **_ar_**
play   fort   scarf
         cord   yarn

My car has a horn.

Blue Level

Sample Dictation Exercises

ir

---

ir   **ar**

fir   part

stir   spark

girl

The bird will chirp.

---

ai   **ir**   **or**

pain   first   sport

     third   sort

Dirt got on my sock.

---

ir   **or**   **i-e**

firm   storm   white

twirl   porch

My shirt is torn.

Road to Reading: A Program for Preventing and Remediating Reading Difficulties by Benita A. Blachman & Darlene M. Tangel

Blue Level

Sample Dictation Exercises

ur

---

ur	**u**
curl	fun
turn	lump
blur	

The burn hurt my hand.

---

or	**ur**	**a**
cord	surf	sad
	burst	
	curb	

The cat has black fur.

---

ar	**ur**	**ee**
art	church	sweet
jar	slurp	

Turn the car to the left.

Blue Level

Sample Dictation Exercises

er

<table>
<tr><td>**<u>e</u>**</td><td>**<u>er</u>**</td></tr>
<tr><td>beg</td><td>herd</td></tr>
<tr><td>sled</td><td>jerk</td></tr>
<tr><td></td><td>her</td></tr>
</table>

I gave her a fern.

<table>
<tr><td>**<u>ar</u>**</td><td>**<u>er</u>**</td><td>**<u>or</u>**</td></tr>
<tr><td>jar</td><td>Bert</td><td>cork</td></tr>
<tr><td></td><td>herd</td><td></td></tr>
<tr><td></td><td>clerk</td><td></td></tr>
</table>

His name is Bert.

Purple Level

Goals for the Purple Level

When the students complete this level, they should be able to do the following:

☆1☆ Read consonant + *le* syllables (e.g., ap**ple**, can**dle**, nee**dle**, bu**gle**).

☆2☆ Read two-syllable words with *y* as a vowel (e.g., funn**y**, pon**y**).

☆3☆ Read one- and two-syllable words with variant sounds of *c* and *g* (e.g., **c**ent, **g**entle).

☆4☆ Read one-syllable words with the patterns *-tch* and *-dge* (e.g., ca**tch**, bri**dge**).

☆5☆ Read selected words in which the base word changes when *-ed* is added (e.g., nodd**ed**, lik**ed**).

☆6☆ Read compound words and multisyllabic words made up of previously learned syllable patterns (e.g., *pineapple, noodle, lawnmower, yardstick, reptile, raisin, equipment*).

Step 1

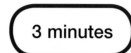

3 minutes

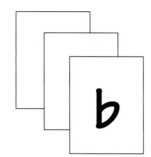

Review Sound–Symbol Correspondences

Materials

 Sound pack cards (sounds for review and new sounds)

Procedures

Use your sound pack of previously learned letter sounds to quickly review selected consonant digraphs, short and long vowels, vowel teams, and vowel + *r* combinations with your students.

Remember the goal is to develop fluency, not boredom.

Step
1

Consonant + *le*

Consonant + *le* cards should be added to the sound pack (e.g., -*ple*, -*dle*, -*tle*, -*ble*, -*fle*, -*gle*, -*kle*, -*zle*, -*cle*).

Explain to the students that they will be learning to read words that end in a consonant letter plus *le* (e.g., ap**ple**, lit**tle**, pud**dle**, ruf**fle**, snug**gle**). The *le* in this pattern always has the /ul/ sound.

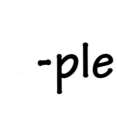

Step 1

Y as a Vowel

Add the red *y* card to the sound pack. Remind the students that (as learned previously in the **Yellow Level**) the *y* can act as a vowel when it comes at the end of a one-syllable word (e.g., *cr**y***). It makes the long /i/ sound as in *cry*.

In this level, explain to the students that *y* also acts as a vowel and makes the long /i/ sound when it comes at the end of a syllable in a multisyllable word (e.g., *c**y**clone, c**y**cle, rec**y**cle*).

Next, in this level, explain to the students that *y* also acts as a vowel when it comes at the end of a two-syllable word. It makes the long /e/ sound as in *bab**y***. Once this concept has been introduced, put two red dots in the upper right corner of the red *y* card. The students should be able to give both the long /i/ sound as in *cr**y*** and the long /e/ sound as in *bab**y***, when they see the red *y* card in this step.

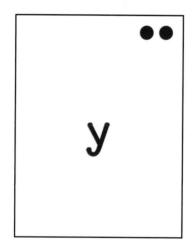

Variant Sounds of c and g

You should also introduce a second sound in the sound pack for c (e.g., **c**ider) and g (e.g., **g**entle). At this point, put a second dot on the c and g cards in the sound pack to remind the students that these letters have two sounds. The students should give both sounds when shown the c or g card.

When c and g are followed by e, i, or y, their sounds change. For example,

- c makes the /s/ sound (e.g., **c**ent, **c**ider, **c**ycle) but also makes the /k/ sound (e.g., **c**at, **c**ut, **c**ot).

- g makes the /j/ sound (e.g., **g**entle, **g**iraffe, **g**ym) but also makes the /g/ sound (e.g., **g**ag, **g**ot, **g**um).

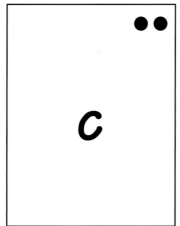
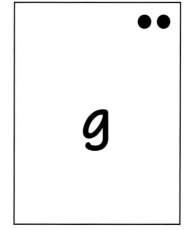

Step 1

Step 2

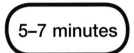

Teach or Review New Decoding Skill

5–7 minutes

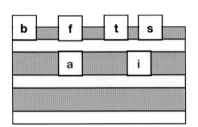

Materials

 Sound board for each student

 Consonant letters and digraphs in the top pocket (only include those needed to make words for a particular lesson)

 Vowel letters and vowel teams in the middle pocket (only include those needed to make words for a particular lesson)

One dry erase board, one dry erase marker, and one eraser for the teacher

Step 2

Procedures

Use the dry erase board to introduce consonant + *le* syllables.

Consonant + *le*

To introduce words with a consonant + *le* syllable, use your dry erase board to help students see the pattern.

- On the first day, write the following consonant + *le* patterns on the dry erase board. (As shown below, draw a line before each consonant + *le* syllable.)

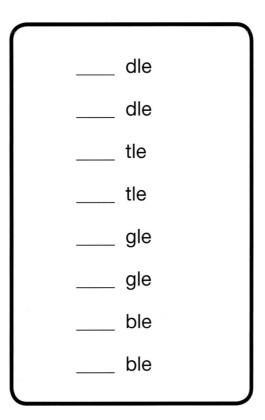

_____ dle

_____ dle

_____ tle

_____ tle

_____ gle

_____ gle

_____ ble

_____ ble

- Read these syllable patterns for the students.

- Next, add a beginning syllable (*can*) to the first consonant + *le* syllable on the dry erase board. Read the first word for the students (*candle*).

Step

2

- Continue to add a beginning closed syllable to each consonant + *le* syllable. As each new word is written, ask one of the students to read the word.

candle

middle

little

rattle

wiggle

giggle

scribble

tumble

- When you have completed the list, ask for volunteers to read the entire list.

The following day, repeat the procedure for introducing the consonant + *le* pattern.

Write the following consonant + *le* patterns on the dry erase board. Draw a line before each consonant + *le* syllable.

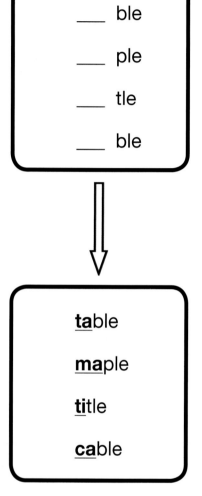

- Read these syllable patterns for the students.

- Next, add the beginning open syllable (*ta*) to the first consonant + *le* syllable on the dry erase board. Read the first word for the students (*table*).

- If the students have difficulty reading the open syllable (*ta*) in the first word, remind the students about open syllables. Open syllables end in one vowel, and the vowel says its name.

- Continue to add the beginning syllable to each consonant + *le* syllable. As each new word is written, ask one of the students to read the word.

Remember that prior to this level, the students have been introduced to open syllable words in two previous levels. In the **Yellow Level**, students learned simple open syllables, such as *he, she, hi, go,* and *my.* In the Green Level, students learned to read two-syllable words, such as *robot* and *minus*, in which the first syllable is an open syllable.

- Clear the dry erase board, and write the following consonant + *le* syllables.

- Read these syllable patterns for the students.

___ tle

___ gle

___ ple

___ ble

Step 2

- Next, add the beginning vowel team syllable (*bee*) to the first consonant + *le* syllable on the dry erase board. Read the first word for the students (*beetle*).

- Continue to add the beginning syllable to each consonant + *le* syllable. As each new word is written, ask one of the students to read the word.

beetle

eagle

purple

marble

You can also put the detached syllables (e.g., lit tle) from the words on individual cards. Mix up the cards and have the students match the syllables to make words.

See the Additional Materials section at the end of this level for lists of words with the consonant + *le* pattern.

> **Please note:** Use the sound boards in this step to reinforce and consolidate previously learned syllable patterns. Feel free to use lists from any of the previous levels to practice the patterns that your students need to review.
>
> The notes you make on your daily lesson plans should guide you in selecting these lists or in creating new ones tailored to the needs of your students.

Step 3

5 minutes

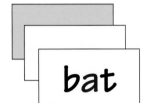

bat

Review Phonetically Regular Words (PRWs) and High Frequency Words (HFWs)

Materials

 Phonetically regular word (PRW) cards (only those words you plan to use in a particular lesson)

 High frequency word (HFW) cards (only those words that you plan to use in a particular lesson)

One dry erase board, one dry erase marker, and one eraser for the teacher

Procedures

The goal of this activity is to develop fluency. The focus is on the phonetically regular words, with a few high frequency words included.

> *Please note: When the students have completed this level, they will have learned all six syllable patterns. This should enable the students to read a greater variety of both single syllable and multisyllable words.*

Step
3

The phonetically regular words (PRWs) should consist of words with the new pattern you are teaching (consonant + *le* syllables).

In addition, the following types of words will be introduced in this step, first on the dry erase board and then written on cards:

- Words with *y* as a vowel at the end of a two-syllable word (e.g., *tid**y***)

- Words with variant sounds of *c* and *g* (e.g., **_c_***ider*, **_g_***entle*)

- Words with *-tch* and *-dge* (e.g., *ca**tch***, *bri**dge***)

- Words in which the base word changes when *-ed* is added (e.g., *nodd**ed***, *lik**ed***)

Words with previously learned syllable patterns (e.g., closed, open, final "e," vowel teams, and vowel + *r*) should also be included in your phonetically regular word cards and reviewed.

Phonetically Regular Words (PRWs)

Consonant + *le* Syllables

Once the students can successfully read words with consonant + *le* that were made on the dry erase board, you can add words with this pattern to your phonetically regular word (PRW) cards.

A starter set of PRWs follows. The Additional Materials section at the end of this level contains more lists of words with consonant + *le* syllables.

Starter Set of Purple Level Phonetically Regular Word (PRW) Cards

Consonant + *le*

-fle	**-tle**	**-kle**	**-ble**	**-cle**
sniffle	beetle	sparkle	bubble	uncle
raffle	turtle		able	
truffle	little		nibble	
	title		table	
	bottle			

-zle	**-ple**	**dle**	**gle**
fizzle	simple	needle	bugle
drizzle	apple	puddle	juggle
puzzle	purple	cradle	eagle
	staple	curdle*	wiggle
	ripple	riddle	
	maple	handle	
		hurdle	

*Do your students know what the word **curdle** means?

If not, this is a good opportunity to expand vocabulary.

Step 3

Remember to look for opportunities to extend vocabulary in each lesson.

Two-Syllable Words with *y* as a Vowel

To introduce two-syllable words that include open and closed syllables and *y* as a vowel (e.g., *funny, silly, tidy, pony, baby*), use the dry erase board.

On the first day, write the following words on the dry erase board and underline the *y,* as shown.

sunn**y**

pupp**y**

sill**y**

tumm**y**

bagg**y**

tedd**y**

- Ask the students what letter is underlined in each word.

- Tell the students that when *y* comes at the end of a two-syllable word, the *y* makes the long /e/ sound, as in *sunny*. (Remind the students that they already know how to break these words into two parts by dividing between the double consonant letters.)

- With your dry erase marker, draw a line between the double letters or draw a curved line under the two parts to remind the students how to "scoop."

sun/ny

- Have the students read the words, reminding them, if necessary, that the *y* makes the long /e/ sound.

- On the next day, repeat the same procedure, selecting six of the following words:

penny	funny	hilly
skinny	fluffy	messy
jelly	fuzzy	mommy
holly	taffy	daddy
yummy	bunny	

Once the students can read these words on the dry erase board, gradually add them to your phonetically regular word cards.

Once students can read words such as *bunny*, use the dry erase board to introduce two-syllable words that end in *y* and begin with an *open* syllable (e.g., *tidy, pony, lady*).

Write the following words on the dry erase board and underline the *y*, as shown

baby

pony

lady

tiny

tidy

lazy

ruby

- Ask the students if they remember what sound *y* makes at the end of a two-syllable word. If they do not remember, tell them it makes the long /e/ sound as in *ba**y***.

- Remind the students that these words are different from the words they read in the previous lesson. These words do *not* have double consonants like the word *fu**nn**y*. These words contain a vowel between two consonants. Students learned how to divide these words in the Green Level. In all of the examples used in this lesson, the words will be divided after the vowel (e.g., ba/by).

- Divide the first word (ba/by), and read it for the students.

- Remind the students that when they divide a word after a vowel, the vowel will have the long sound (says its name). This is an open syllable.

- Demonstrate again by breaking the next word after the vowel (po/ny) and reading it for the students.

- Divide the rest of the words (*lady, tiny, tidy, lazy, ruby*) after the vowel, and have the students read these words.

Step
3

Once the students can read these words on the dry erase board, gradually add the words to your phonetically regular word (PRW) cards.

See the Additional Materials section at the end of this level for lists of two-syllable words ending in *y*.

Words with Variant Sounds of *c* and *g*

In Step 1 of this level, students were introduced to a second sound for *c* and *g.*

> When *c* and *g* are followed by *e, i,* or *y,* their sounds change. For example,
>
> - *c* makes the /s/ sound (e.g., **c**ent, **c**ider, **c**ycle), but it also makes the /k/ sound (e.g., **c**at, **c**ut, **c**ot)
>
> - *g* makes the /j/ sound (e.g., **g**entle, **g**iraffe, **g**ym), but it also makes the /g/ sound (e.g., **g**ag, **g**ot, **g**um).

Tell the students that when *c* and *g* are followed by *e, i, or y,* their sounds change. The *c* makes the sound of /s/ as in **c**ent, and *g* makes the sound of /j/ as in **g**em. These are sometimes called *soft* /c/ and *soft* /g/.

- To practice words with soft /c/, put the following words on the dry erase board, and underline the vowel that comes after the *c,* as shown below:

> c**e**nt
>
> fac**e**
>
> fenc**e**
>
> pric**e**
>
> c**i**rcle
>
> c**i**ty

- Ask the students if the underlined vowel is an *e, i,* or *y.*

Step
3

- Next, ask the students what sound the *c* should make, and have the students read the words.

For more challenging practice, put the following words on the dry erase board, and underline the vowel that comes after the *c,* as shown below:

c<u>a</u>n

c<u>o</u>ne

danc<u>e</u>

nic<u>e</u>

c<u>i</u>rc<u>u</u>s

- Next, ask the students what sound the *c* should make in each word, and have them read the words.

- To practice words with soft /g/, put the following words on the dry erase board, and underline the vowel that comes after the *g,* as shown below:

g<u>e</u>m

ag<u>e</u>

pag<u>e</u>

hug<u>e</u>

stag<u>e</u>

g<u>e</u>ntle

marg<u>i</u>n

- Ask the students if the underlined vowel is an *e*, *i*, or *y*.

- Next, ask the students what sound the *g* should make, and have the students read the words.

- To further illustrate the different sounds of *g*, you can write the following pairs on the dry erase board:

> **wag..............wage**
>
> **hug..............huge**
>
> **stag.............stage**
>
> **lung............lunge**

See the Additional Materials section at the end of this level for lists of one- and two-syllable words with soft /c/ and /g/.

Words with -tch and -dge (a Special Case)

Write the following words on the dry erase board to introduce *-tch*:

> itch
>
> catch
>
> pitch
>
> scratch
>
> stretch

- First, read the words for the students.

- Next, have the students read the words.

- Ask the students which letter is underlined in each word.

- Tell the students that to make the /ch/ sound at the end of a one-syllable word with a short vowel, the short vowel needs support, and *t* is added right after the vowel and before the *ch*.

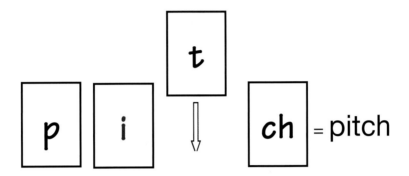

Please note: There are a few exceptions to this special case. The high frequency words that the students learned in previous levels (e.g., su*ch*, mu*ch*, whi*ch*) do not follow this rule.

Our purpose in introducing this special case is to draw the students' attention to the extra letter when they are **reading** and to give teachers an explanation of why the extra letters are needed. Students at this level may not yet internalize and use this rule for spelling, even though they **can read the words**.

Step
3

Write the following words on the dry erase board to introduce *-dge*:

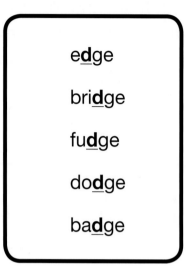

edge

bridge

fudge

dodge

badge

- First, read the words for the students.

- Next, have the students read the words.

- Then, ask the students which letter is underlined in each word.

- Tell the students that to get the /j/ sound at the end of a one-syllable word with a short vowel, the short vowel needs support, and *d* is added before the *ge*.

| b | r | i | d | g | e | = bridge |

Words in Which the Base Word Changes When *-ed* Is Added

It is a good idea to introduce words in which the base word changes when *-ed* is added in this step of the lesson.

Doubling the Final Consonant

- To introduce words in which the base word changes when *-ed* is added, write the following words on the dry erase board.

> no**d**
>
> ba**t**
>
> ste**p**
>
> hu**g**
>
> ski**p**

- Have the students practice reading these base words.

- Next, add *-ed* to each base word, read the words for the students, and ask the students what letter is doubled.

> no**dd**ed
>
> ba**tt**ed
>
> ste**pp**ed
>
> hu**gg**ed
>
> ski**pp**ed

- Finally, have the students read each of the words.

> **Please note:** For one-syllable words that end in **one vowel** followed by **one consonant** (e.g., *step*), double the final consonant when adding an ending that begins with a vowel (e.g., *-ed, -ing*). For example, double the final consonant when adding *-ed* and *-ing* to *step* (*stepped, stepping*), but do not double the final consonant when adding *-ed* and *-ing* to *lift* (e.g., *lifted, lifting*).
>
> Depending on the age and ability of your students, you may or may not choose to explain the doubling rule. At this point, it is more important that young students can read these words when they encounter them in text.

Dropping Final "e"

- To introduce words in which the base word changes when *-ed* is added, write the following words on the dry erase board.

like

joke

hope

time

use

dance

- First, have the students practice reading these base words.

- Next, add *-ed* to each base word, read the words for the students, and ask the students what letter was dropped.

liked

joked

hoped

timed

used

danced

- If the students do not know what letter was dropped or they answer incorrectly, demonstrate on your dry erase board. Write the following:

lik**e** + **e**d = liked

- Explain to the students that the final "e" in *like* is dropped when the *-ed* is added.

- Finally, have the students read each of the words.

Please note: For one-syllable words that end in "e" (e.g., *like*), drop the final "e" before adding an ending that begins with a vowel (e.g., *-ed, -ing*). For example, drop the final "e" when adding *-ed* and *-ing* to *like* (*lik**ed**, lik**ing***) but not when adding *-ly* (*like**ly***).

Again, depending on the age and ability of your students, you may or may not choose to explain the rule for dropping final "e." At this point, it is more important that young students can read these words when they encounter them in text.

Include words with the *-ed* ending in your phonetically regular word (PRW) cards in this step.

Remember to also include compound words and multisyllabic words made up of previously learned syllable patterns (e.g., *pineapple*, *noodle, lawnmower, yardstick, reptile, raisin, equipment*) in your phonetically regular word cards for this level.

Students can now read all six syllable types, and they need opportunities to practice these patterns in more challenging combinations.

High Frequency Words (HFWs) 251–300

The following high frequency words (HFWs) from Fry and Kress (2006) can be taught and added to your word card pack. You might want to pretest the students on these HFWs at this level and create an individualized list of HFWs that the students still need to learn. A High Frequency Word Assessment form for the Purple Level and individual word cards are included on the CD-ROM ⊙.

important	*until	children	*side	*feet	*car	*mile
*night	*walk	*quite	*see	*began	*grow	*took
*river	four	carry	*state	once	*book	here
*stop	*without	second	*later	*miss	idea	enough
*eat	*face	watch	*far	Indian	*really	almost
*let	above	girl	sometimes	mountain	*cut	young
*talk	*soon	*list	song	*being	leave	family
*it's						

Adapted from *The Reading Teacher's Book of Lists, Fifth Edition,* by E.B. Fry and J. Kress
© 2006 Jossey-Bass. Reprinted with permission from John Wiley & Sons, Inc.

*Students learned to decode words written in red, orange, yellow, green, and blue during the Red, Orange, Yellow, Green, and Blue levels in this program, respectively.

Step
3

Once each high frequency word has been mastered by most of the students, you might want to file the word in the back of a high frequency word box in alphabetical order. Review these words on a regular basis in Step 3 of your lesson to make sure that the students remember them.

As is evident from the many high frequency words in this level that appear color-coded in the chart on the previous page, students who have learned the six syllable types can use their decoding skill to read 60% of the high frequency words included in this level. This greatly reduces the number of high frequency words that might otherwise need to be memorized.

An Important Note About Developing Fluency

Remember, the overall goal of this activity is to develop fluency at the word level. A hallmark of good readers is the ability to read both accurately and fluently.

To help students develop fluency, you will need to have the students read the words more than once.

Activities for Developing Fluency

- When the students read the words for the second time, try using an hourglass to encourage the students to move more quickly. The students like to see how many words they can read before the sand runs out.

- Use a stopwatch with the group and have the students see how long it takes to read all the words in the card pack for that day.

- Students can also use the hourglass and stopwatch while working in pairs. Each student tries to read his or her words more quickly than during his or her previous reading. In this way, the students are encouraged to improve their own times and not compete with each other.

Step
3

Step 4  Read Orally in Context

15–20 minutes

Materials

Selected decodable readers from previous levels

Selected books/stories from your classroom or school library or basal program (suggested book titles appear in Appendix B)

Procedures

At this level, students should be able to read a wide variety of texts, such as chapter books, nonfiction, poetry, and plays, with corrective feedback to develop fluency.

As noted in the *Report of the National Reading Panel* (National Institute of Child Health and Human Development, 2000), "Fluent readers are able to read orally with speed, accuracy, and proper expression. Fluency is one of several critical factors for reading comprehension" (p. 11).

Step 4

Note About Decodable Books for the Purple Level

We are not providing a decodable book chart for this level. The students have now been introduced to all six syllable patterns. *Feel free to have the students reread any of the decodable books or sample reading sentences from previous levels that reinforce patterns your students need to practice for accuracy and fluency.*

Some decodable series might have readers that reinforce the consonant + *le* pattern taught in this level (e.g., *The Little Skunk*, Primary Phonics, Set 4, Book 4). These books could be used to further reinforce this pattern.

Your daily lesson plans should help you identify the patterns that you need to review during oral reading with your students.

An Important Note About Building Fluency

Although many of your students will be becoming more fluent as they progress through the levels of the program, others will still require opportunities for *frequent repeated readings* of text with corrective feedback to build fluency.

Step
4

An Important Note About Selecting Books

Students who have reached this level need ample opportunity to consolidate their skills and to continue to build accuracy and fluency by reading a wide variety of texts throughout the week.

Many students may now be proficient enough to read most of the text in grade appropriate trade books, such as chapter books, nonfiction, poetry, and plays. Other students may continue to need more review or reteaching of previously presented material, as well as more support from the teacher (e.g., needing the teacher to supply unknown words or alternating reading when texts become longer, as in chapter books).

Appendix B contains some titles of trade books that many students will be able to read successfully. ***Again, feel free to substitute your favorite books for students reading at this level.***

Step
4

Step 5 Dictation

5–7 minutes

Materials

Dictation notebook for each student

Pencil

One dry erase board, one dry erase marker, and one eraser for the teacher

Procedures

At this level, the format changes for dictation because you will be dictating words with two or more syllables. Vowel headings are no longer used. Determine how many words you want to dictate. We recommend six to eight words plus one or two sentences. Have the students number their papers accordingly.

Examples of notebook dictation pages:

---

1. table   4. candle
2. maple   5. simple
3. cable   6. turtle
4. pineapple

Put the candle on the table.

---

1. apple   4. bottle
2. little   5. puddle
3. puzzle   6. rattlesnake

The puzzle was simple.

- Check each student's work, and help him or her correct errors.

- If the student continues to have difficulty, demonstrate for the student on *your* dry erase board, have the student copy the word correctly, and move on to the next word.

- At the end of the dictation lesson, have the students read aloud the words and sentences they have written.

Refer to the Additional Materials section at the end of this level for more lists of words with consonant + *le* to help you create additional consonant + *le* dictation exercises.

Step
5

Please note: In future dictation lessons, you have the option of having students set up the pages with vowel headings when you are reviewing one-syllable words from previous levels.

You can use the list format described on the previous page when you dictate consonant + *le* syllables, as well as when you dictate compound words (e.g., *pineapple, yardstick*) and multisyllable words (e.g., *reptile, noodle, fantastic*) made up of previously learned syllable types.

Refer to the notes on your daily lesson plan to decide what you need to review and the best format to use.

Step
5

Additional Materials

Purple Level

Phonetically Regular Word Lists (consonant + *le*)

closed/ *consonant + le*		*closed/* *consonant + le*	
apple	little	candle	tumble
puddle	puzzle	simple	handle
bottle	nibble	bundle	sample
pebble	middle	dimple	grumble
juggle	drizzle	fumble	
rattle	snuggle		
riddle	struggle		
wiggle	scribble		

Purple Level

Phonetically Regular Word Lists (consonant + *le*)

vowel team/ consonant + le	*open/ consonant + le*	*vowel + r/ consonant + le*
beetle	able	circle
eagle	table	turtle
needle	title	purple
steeple	maple	gurgle
	cable	hurdle
		marble
		startle
		sparkle

Purple Level

Phonetically Regular Word Lists

(two-syllable words ending with *y*)

teddy	fuzzy	bumpy	lazy
mommy	bunny	frisky	baby
daddy	funny	lumpy	pony
tummy	silly	tricky	tidy
baggy	hilly	dusty	tiny
sloppy	skinny	study	lady
puppy	messy	sleepy	ruby
penny	fluffy	rainy	duty
yummy	sunny	creamy	
holly	happy	chalky	
jelly	hobby		
taffy	Bobby		

Purple Level

Phonetically Regular Word Lists

(one-syllable words with soft /c/ and /g/)

soft /c/			soft /g/	
face	cent	since	gem	urge
lace	cell	dance	age	forge
brace	clinch	fence	cage	barge
place	voice	prince	page	large
space	choice	chance	wage	charge
ice	peace	glance*	stage	gorge
mice		sauce	huge	splurge*
nice		force	germ	
price			cringe	
rice			fringe	
slice			hinge	
twice			twinge	
spice			bulge	
spruce			lunge	

*Do the students know what the words **glance** and **splurge** mean?

Remember to look for other opportunities to extend vocabulary in each lesson.

Purple Level

Phonetically Regular Word Lists

(two-syllable words with soft /c/ and /g/)

soft /c/		soft /g/
center	advice	angel
cider	advance	challenge
circle	concert	digest
circus	decide	gentle
city	decent	gender
cycle	excite	gerbil
cyclone	enforce	ginger
Cinderella*	fancy	magic
	mercy	margin
	pencil	suggest
	princess	teenager*
	recess	
	sentence	
	silence	

*Challenge words are more than two syllables.

 Road to Reading: A Program for Preventing and Remediating Reading Difficulties by Benita A. Blachman & Darlene M. Tangel

Purple Level

Phonetically Regular Word Lists

(one-syllable words with -*tch* and -*dge*)

-*tch*		-*dge*
batch	thatch	ridge
notch	hitchhike*	bridge
catch	pitcher*	hedge
glitch	witch	dodge
latch	latch	edge
blotch	etch	lodge
match	switch	wedge
scratch		fudge
pitch		badge
hopscotch*		ledge
itch		judge
fetch		smudge
hatch		budge
ditch		pledge
		grudge

*Challenge words are two syllables.

Appendix A
Sample Lesson Plans

This section contains **three sample lesson plans** from **each level of the program**.

- The first plan (numbered 1) represents a lesson that you might teach **early** in each level.

- The second plan (numbered 2) represents a lesson that you might teach when you are in the **middle** of each level.

- The third lesson (numbered 3) represents a lesson you might teach when you are nearing the **end** of each level.

> To get you started, the three sample lessons for the Red Level include lists that come **directly** from words that you will find in the text of the Red Level or in the Additional Materials section of the Red Level.

Remember, before your first lesson you will want to give students the letter–sound assessment that can be found on the CD-ROM ⊙. Use this assessment to determine which letter names and letter sounds your students know and which ones they need to learn.

The steps below refer to the items on the *first sample Red Level lesson* (Red 1) and show you how the program can be used to help you create your lesson plans.

1. **Step 1** includes a few letters to review (based on the assessment), as well as a new letter to introduce.

2. The **Step 2** sound board list comes from the Additional Materials section at the end of the Red Level (p. 63).

3. The **Step 3** phonetically regular words (PRWs) come from the ***Starter Set of PRW cards*** in the Red Level (p. 30) and the high frequency words (HFWs) come from the ***HFW Chart*** (p. 33) in the Red Level.

4. The **Step 4** book comes from the Red Level ***Decodable Book Chart*** (p. 43). As always, you are free to substitute other decodable books that are available to you.

5. The **Step 5** words for dry erase board dictation come from the dictation lists in the Red Level (p. 51).

All of the words in each of the steps of the sample Red Level lessons come **directly** from lists found either in the Red Level text or in the Additional Materials section of the Red Level.

> **Please note: The sample lessons for each of the other levels of the program do not necessarily use the prepared lists found in the book.**

- When you create your first lessons for a particular level, you may find it helpful to use lists from the text or Additional Materials sections, as we did in the sample lessons for the Red Level.

- As you adjust your lessons to meet the needs of your students, you may want to create your own lists (e.g., words for the sound board) that focus on a particular skill that your students need to learn or review.

> After reviewing the sample lessons, you will find an instruction page (p. 428) titled **How to Create a Daily Lesson Plan** to use as a guide when creating your own daily lesson plans.

DAILY LESSON PLAN

1. Review sound–symbol correspondences					Notes:
a	t	b	n	*i* (new)	"i" is new today!
r	p	m	f	c	It will not appear in other steps of this lesson.

2. Teach or review new decoding skill (sound board)

Letters needed: a, t, r, c, p, n, b

				Notes:
at	rat	cat	cap	Each day, list the letters needed. Remember, students change only one sound at a time (at → rat → cat).
nap	nab	tab		

3. Review phonetically regular words (PRWs) and high frequency words (HFWs)

PRWs			HFWs	Notes:
mat	mad		the	Use fewer PRWs for the first few lessons. Work up to 12 PRWs.
pat			on	
tab			is	
fan				
cap				

4. Read orally in context (decodable text or trade book)

Choose a decodable book focusing on short /a/ without blends or digraphs, such as Primary Phonics (PP 1-1), *Mac and Tab*.

Notes:

5. Dictation (PRWs and sentence with PRWs and HFWs)

at	mat	map	tap		

Notes:
Use a dry erase board. Sentences are not dictated at this level.

DAILY LESSON PLAN

1. Review sound–symbol correspondences					Notes:
a	e	i	o	u	
b	d	c	m	qu	
h	x	y	v	r	

2. Teach or review new decoding skill (sound board)

Letters needed: t, e, n, p, o, h, i

Notes:

ten	pen	pet	pot
hot	hop	hip	

3. Review phonetically regular words (PRWs) and high frequency words (HFWs)

Notes:
Select words with all short vowels from the starter set of PRW lists.

PRWs			HFWs
fan	rob	red	you
hat	nut	ten	have
lip	bus		was
kid	fed		
hot	jet		

4. Read orally in context (decodable text or trade book)

Choose a decodable book focusing on short vowels without blends or digraphs, such as Steck-Vaughn (SV 1-6), *Fun in the Sun*.

Notes:
Read short /e/ book tomorrow.

5. Dictation (PRWs and sentence with PRWs and HFWs)

Headings needed: a, i, u

Notes:
Use notebook dictation.

map	mud	lid	pig	up	

The pup is in the mud.

DAILY LESSON PLAN

1. Review sound–symbol correspondences					Notes:
a	e	i	o	u	"-ck" is new today!
p	sh	th	ch	ck	It will not appear in other steps of this lesson.
f	j	r	w	y	

2. Teach or review new decoding skill (sound board)

Notes: Add "-ck" to Step 2 tomorrow.

Letters needed: i, o, l, p, sh, h, ch, n

lip	ship	shop	hop
chop	chip	chin	

3. Review phonetically regular words (PRWs) and high frequency words (HFWs)

Notes: Keep the word "said" in pack all week.

PRWs			HFWs
bug	such	chat	said
fish	jet	thud	were
bath	shed		they
thin	chip		
ship	web		

4. Read orally in context (decodable text or trade book)

Notes:

Choose a decodable book focusing on short vowels without blends or digraphs, such as Primary Phonics (PP 1-10), *The Wig.*

5. Dictation (PRWs and sentence with PRWs and HFWs)

Notes: Remember to use headings in dictation notebooks. Spell HFWs for the students if needed.

Headings needed: a, u, e

shed	dash	hush	cap		

I will shut up the shed.

DAILY LESSON PLAN

1. Review sound–symbol correspondences

a	e	i	o	u
f	l	s	ch	th
h	y	x	ck	sh

Notes:

Remember to review all short vowels.

2. Teach or review new decoding skill (sound board)

Letters needed: i, a, e, h, l, l, p, s, s, t, j, f, f, J

hill	pill	pal	pass
pat	pet	jet	Jeff

Notes:

You will need two of each of the letters l, s, f, and you will need a capital J.

3. Review phonetically regular words (PRWs) and high frequency words (HFWs)

PRWs			HFWs
fill	fish	Nick	there
gum	neck	shell	how
check	chill		what
tell	thick		
yell	wag		

Notes:

Review HFWs from previous level.

4. Read orally in context (decodable text or trade book)

Choose a decodable book focusing on short vowels without blends or digraphs, such as More Primary Phonics (MPP M1-3), *The Van and the Hot Rod.*

Notes:

5. Dictation (PRWs and sentence with PRWs and HFWs)

Headings needed: i, e, o

hop	chick	peck	this	rod	

Rush to pack the sack.

Notes:

DAILY LESSON PLAN

1. Review sound–symbol correspondences					Notes:
a	e	i	o	u	Remember, blends are introduced in Step 2 (not Step 1).
f	g	l	ch	ck	
c	s	r	sh	th	

2. Teach or review new decoding skill (sound board)

Letters needed: a, i, l, s, p, m, k

lip	slip	slim	skim
skip	sip	sap	slap

Notes:
Remember, each letter of the blend is written on a separate card (e.g., [s][l])

3. Review phonetically regular words (PRWs) and high frequency words (HFWs)

PRWs			HFWs
block	glad	glass	many
flat	blush	mop	would
led	flop		could
clap	clock		
cliff	flush		

Notes:

4. Read orally in context (decodable text or trade book)

Have students read Sample Reading Sentences with "l" blends (see Additional Materials section, p. 120).

Notes:
Today, use sentences to reinforce words with short vowels and blends.

5. Dictation (PRWs and sentence with PRWs and HFWs)

Headings needed: o, u, e

block	glum	led	club	blob

The flip-flop is black.

Notes:
Remember, use vowel headings for dictation.

Orange 2

414

DAILY LESSON PLAN

1. Review sound–symbol correspondences

a	e	i	o	u
b	r	m	ch	th
w	v	t	sh	ck

Notes:

2. Teach or review new decoding skill (sound board)

Letters needed: a, e, u, b, n, d, h, s, t, m, p, t, l

bend	band	hand	*stand
*stamp	stump	*stunt	*blunt

Notes:
*These words require two changes.

3. Review phonetically regular words (PRWs) and high frequency words (HFWs)

PRWs			HFWs
print	twist	help	first
plump	spent	land	who
brisk	grand		come
belt	blend		
shift	shelf		

Notes:

4. Read orally in context (decodable text or trade book)

Choose a decodable book with short vowels and blends, such as Bob Books Level B (BB B2-2), Bump.

Notes:
Reread this or another easy book for fluency.

5. Dictation (PRWs and sentence with PRWs and HFWs)

Headings needed: e, u

send	hunt	help	tent	junk	

The plump cats will tip the trash can.

Notes:

DAILY LESSON PLAN

1. Review sound–symbol correspondences

a	e	i	o	u
a_e	i_e	o_e	ch	ck
c	s	r	sh	th

Notes:

"o_e" is new today!

It will not appear in other steps in this lesson.

Yellow

1

2. Teach or review new decoding skill (sound board)

Letters needed: *a, i, e, m, t, k, b, d*

dim	dime	time	tame
take	bake	bike	bite

Notes:

Use only final "e" words without blends in early Yellow Level *lessons.*

---

mat

3. Review phonetically regular words (PRWs) and high frequency words (HFWs)

PRWs			HFWs
hid	skip	dime	may
late	cave	wade	part
mine	cliff		new
mad	same		
base	hive		

Notes:

---

4. Read orally in context (decodable text or trade book)

Choose a decodable book focusing on the final "e" patterns that have been taught, such as Primary Phonics (PP 2-2), The Big Game.

Notes:

---

5. Dictation (PRWs and sentence with PRWs and HFWs)

Headings needed: *a_e, a*

stand	gaze	sale	game	flap	

Hide the dime in the safe.

Notes:

1. Review sound–symbol correspondences

a	e	i	o	u
a_e	i_e	e_e	u_e	o_e
ch	sh	th	ck	y

Notes:

Yellow
2

2. Teach or review new decoding skill (sound board)

Letters needed: s, t, e, v, o, w, a, d, g, l, i, b, r

stove	wove	wave	wade
glade	glide	bride	ride

Notes:
Some words now include blends.

3. Review phonetically regular words (PRWs) and high frequency words (HFWs)

PRWs			HFWs
spin	drove	smile	know
broke	shin	state	very
flute	snack	frame	great
glob	chop	speck	where
plate	stove	made	too

Notes:

4. Read orally in context (decodable text or trade book)

Choose a decodable book focusing on final "e" patterns, with or without blends, such as Primary Phonics (PP 2-3), *The Joke.*

Notes:

5. Dictation (PRWs and sentence with PRWs and HFWs)

Headings needed: a_e, o_e, a

spoke	flake	slope	stale	stamp	

Dave broke a bone in his hand.

Notes:

DAILY LESSON PLAN

1. Review sound–symbol correspondences

a	e	i	o	u
a_e	i_e	e_e	u_e••	o_e
ch	sh	th	ck	r

Notes:

Review both sounds of "u_e" (as in "tune" and "use").

2. Teach or review new decoding skill (sound board)

Letters needed: h, i, d, e, s, l, m, y

hi	hid	hide	slide
slid	slim	slime	sly

Notes:

Discuss how vowel sounds change in different syllable types (open, closed, final "e").

3. Review phonetically regular words (PRWs) and high frequency words (HFWs)

PRWs			HFWs
she	bobsled	sunrise	through
go	baseline	backpack	before
fly	inside	uphill	right
try	tadpole	pancake	any
cannot	catfish	sunlamp	old

Notes:

Remember, if your students are not ready for compound words, do not include them. Substitute one-syllable PRWs.

4. Read orally in context (decodable text or trade book)

Choose a decodable book focusing on final "e" patterns, with or without blends, such as Steck-Vaughn (SV 2-5), *Miss Duke's Mule*.

Notes:

5. Dictation (PRWs and sentence with PRWs and HFWs)

Headings needed: i_e, u_e, i

stripe	cute	twin	flute	spine	

The catfish and tadpole swam in a lake.

Notes:

Remind the students that they know two sounds for "u_e" (as in "tune" and "use").

DAILY LESSON PLAN

1. Review sound–symbol correspondences					Notes:
a	e	i	o	u	"ea" is new today (as in "seal")!
ai	oa	ee	ea	t	It will not appear in other steps of this
s	p	m	r	qu	lesson.

2. Teach or review new decoding skill (sound board)

Notes:

Letters needed: f, *ee*, l, *ai*, *oa*, c, t, b, e

feel	fail	foal	coal
coat	boat	bet	bait

3. Review phonetically regular words (PRWs) and high frequency words (HFWs)

Notes: Substitute review words from previous lessons as needed (e.g., *nut*, *ride*).

PRWs			HFWs
need	week	loaf	also
sail	keep	toad	small
main	plane	melt	want
soap	nail	bait	around
mine	classmate	cupcake	put

4. Read orally in context (decodable text or trade book)

Notes:

Choose a decodable book focusing on vowel teams that have been taught, such as Primary Phonics (PP 2-5), *The Bee*.

5. Dictation (PRWs and sentence with PRWs and HFWs)

Notes: Substitute easier words for vowel team words in the sentence if needed (e.g., Lee will ride the red bike.)

Headings needed: *ee*, *oa*, e

peek	met	oat	feet	belt	loan

Lee will weep and moan.

1. Review sound–symbol correspondences

a	e	i	o	u
ai	oa	ee	oe	ay
ie	a_e	o_e	i_e	ow

Notes:

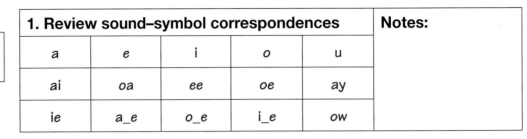

2. Teach or review new decoding skill (sound board)

Letters needed: *oa, k, c, r, ee, p, ow, f, l, n, o, ck*

oak	*croak	*crock	*creek
creep	*crow	*flow	flown

Notes:

These words require two changes.

Green 2

3. Review phonetically regular words (PRWs) and high frequency words (HFWs)

PRWs			HFWs
faith	throw	speed	does
grape	snail	spray	because
swim	seaside	reach	move
speck	coach	rowboat	here
trade	smile	scrape	different

Notes:

4. Read orally in context (decodable text or trade book)

Choose a decodable book focusing on Group I vowel teams with or without blends, such as More Primary Phonics (MPP M2-9), *Rose and Weed*.

Notes:

5. Dictation (PRWs and sentence with PRWs and HFWs)

Headings needed: *ai, ea, o_e*

brain	dream	home	trail	beach	sneak

The snail left a trail of slime.

Notes:

DAILY LESSON PLAN

1. Review sound–symbol correspondences

a	e	i	o	u
ou	oo••	ow••	au	ea••
aw	a_e	ew	oi	oy

Notes:

The vowel team "ea" (as in "head") is new today. Put two dots on the card and review both sounds.

2. Teach or review new decoding skill (sound board)

Letters needed: ou, t, sh, oo, l, k, b, r, oi, c, oy

out	shout	*shook	look
*brook	*broil	*coil	*coy

Notes:

*These words require two changes.

3. Review phonetically regular words (PRWs) and high frequency words (HFWs)

PRWs			HFWs
school	chow	flame	kind
ploy	pool	chew	picture
spoil	toy	plate	again
flew	coin	crawl	should
felt	drawn	spend	answer

Notes:

4. Read orally in context (decodable text or trade book)

Choose a decodable book focusing on Group I or Group II vowel teams with or without blends, such as Primary Phonics (PP 5-6), *The Shy Tiger*.

Notes:

5. Dictation (PRWs and sentence with PRWs and HFWs)

Headings needed: oi, oy, o

moist	joy	stop	spoil	Troy	broil

Roy will not show me that coin.

Notes:

DAILY LESSON PLAN

1. Review sound–symbol correspondences

a	e	i	oo••	aw
au	oi	ar	or	ea••
e_e	i_e	a_e	oy	ew

Notes:

"or" is new today!

It will not appear in other steps of the lesson.

2. Teach or review new decoding skill (sound board)

Letters needed: *c, ar, t, ch, m, h, p, sh, k*

car	cart	chart	charm
harm	harp	sharp	shark

Notes:

3. Review phonetically regular words (PRWs) and high frequency words (HFWs)

PRWs			HFWs
jar	start	park	near
card	meal	teach	learn
clean	Mark	cheat	every
hard	farm	cream	country
catnip	cobweb	himself	father

Notes:

4. Read orally in context (decodable text or trade book)

Choose a book from the trade book list or a decodable book (if needed), such as Primary Phonics (PP 4–6), *The Go-Cart.*

Notes:

5. Dictation (PRWs and sentence with PRWs and HFWs)

Headings needed: *ar, ea, oi*

yarn	harp	broil	team	March	clean

The hen is in the barnyard.

Notes:

Blue 1

DAILY LESSON PLAN

1. Review sound–symbol correspondences					Notes:
a	e	i	o	u	
ar	or	ir	ea••	oi	
e_e	u_e••	ee	ay	ou	

2. Teach or review new decoding skill (sound board)

Notes:

Letters needed: *d, ar, t, t, ir, sh, or, p, s, o*

dirt	shirt	short	sport
spot	pot	part	start

3. Review phonetically regular words (PRWs) and high frequency words (HFWs)

Notes:

PRWs			HFWs
sink	sank	storm	thought
third	drink	torch	something
birth	skunk	thank	story
junk	skirt	stain	along
stay	foil	sport	city

4. Read orally in context (decodable text or trade book)

Notes:

Select a book from the trade book list or a decodable book (if needed), such as Primary Phonics (PP 4-7), *The Lost Horse.*

5. Dictation (PRWs and sentence with PRWs and HFWs)

Notes:

Headings needed: *or, ar, a*

fork	scarf	plant	stars	stamps	torch

The storm blew in from the north.

Blue
2

423

DAILY LESSON PLAN

1. Review sound–symbol correspondences

a	e	i	o	u
ar	or	ir	ur	er
oi	oy	ew	aw	au

Notes:

2. Teach or review new decoding skill (sound board)

Letters needed: or, k, p, ar, t, s, ur, n, ch, ch, t

turn	churn	church	porch
pork	park	stark	start

Notes:

3. Review phonetically regular words (PRWs) and high frequency words (HFWs)

PRWs			HFWs
church	draw	stern	often
chirp	burn	jerk	together
skirt	grew	surf	group
perk	burst	birthmark	both
shrunk	drank	think	example

Notes:

4. Read orally in context (decodable text or trade book)

Choose a book from the trade book lists or a decodable book (if needed), such as Primary Phonics (PP 4-9), *The Birdfeeder.*

Notes:

5. Dictation (PRWs and sentence with PRWs and HFWs)

Headings needed: or, ur, er

storm	curl	perch	snort	thorn	turn

My big thirst made me slurp.

Notes:

DAILY LESSON PLAN

1. Review sound–symbol correspondences					Notes:
a	e	i	o	u	Remember to review the two sounds of "ea" (as in "eat" and "head").
ar	ir	or	er	ur	
ie	ea●●	-tle	-ble	-dle	

2. Teach or review new decoding skill (sound board)				Notes:
Letters needed: None. Use the dry erase board.				Remember to use the dry erase board and not the sound board.
little	rattle	wiggle	stumble	
candle	sample	thimble	middle	

3. Review phonetically regular words (PRWs) and high frequency words (HFWs)				Notes:
PRWs			**HFWs**	
bundle	handle	termite	four	
forbid	simple	tumble	important	
river	silver	riddle	children	
pebble	winter	blurt	carry	
ripple	puzzle	hurt	once	

4. Read orally in context (decodable text or trade book)	Notes:
Select trade books from various genres or read a book that reinforces a pattern your students need to practice.	

5. Dictation (PRWs and sentence with PRWs and HFWs)						Notes:
Headings needed: none						Use a numbered list format for dictating two-syllable words (more like a traditional spelling test).
babble	apple	candle	bottle	tumble	middle	
The cattle wobble and jiggle in the mud.						

DAILY LESSON PLAN

1. Review sound–symbol correspondences

-dle	-ple	-gle	-fle	-ble
-tle	-kle	ar	ur	y●●
ou	oo●●	ea●●	o	ow●●

Notes:

Put two dots on the red "y" card to indicate the two different sounds (as in "cry" and "baby").

2. Teach or review new decoding skill (sound board)

Letters needed: None. Use the dry erase board.

giggle	cable	table	maple
tumble	title	scribble	cable

Notes:

Remember to use the dry erase board and not the sound board.

3. Review phonetically regular words (PRWs) and high frequency words (HFWs)

PRWs			HFWs
snuggle	ruffle	cry	second
yummy	staple	cradle	idea
funny	lazy	maple	enough
sly	baby	spry	watch
couch	thread	spooky	almost

Notes:

Discuss the two sounds of "y" as a vowel.

4. Read orally in context (decodable text or trade book)

Select trade books from various genres.

Notes:

5. Dictation (PRWs and sentence with PRWs and HFWs)

Headings needed: none

sleepy	staple	cry	table	rainy	bubble

The jelly bean is yummy.

Notes:

Remember to use a numbered list format.

DAILY LESSON PLAN

1. Review sound–symbol correspondences

-kle	-zle	-fle	c••	g••
or	er	ar	ur	ir
aw	ew	ow••	o	y••

Notes:
Remember to review both sounds when a letter card has two dots.

2. Teach or review new decoding skill (sound board)

Letters needed: None. Use the dry erase board.

able	puzzle	eagle	purple
sparkle	nibble	noodle	needle

Notes:
Remember to use the dry erase board and not the sound board.

3. Review phonetically regular words (PRWs) and high frequency words (HFWs)

PRWs			HFWs
tornado	waxy	cell	mountain
cone	price	fantastic	song
crunchy	germ	cent	young
pitch	straw	chew	above
snowy	fudge	twice	family

Notes:

4. Read orally in context (decodable text or trade book)

Select trade books from various genres.

Notes:

5. Dictation (PRWs and sentence with PRWs and HFWs)

Headings needed: none

reptile	noodle	pineapple	lawnmower	tornado	fantastic

My backpack is packed with schoolbooks.

Notes:
Remember to use a numbered list format.

Purple
3

HOW TO CREATE A DAILY LESSON PLAN

This page explains an important procedure to use when creating lesson plans.

> When a new vowel is first introduced in Step 1, it is not included in the rest of the steps in that lesson. As illustrated below, the new vowel is gradually "pulled through" the five steps of the lesson as the skill is mastered.

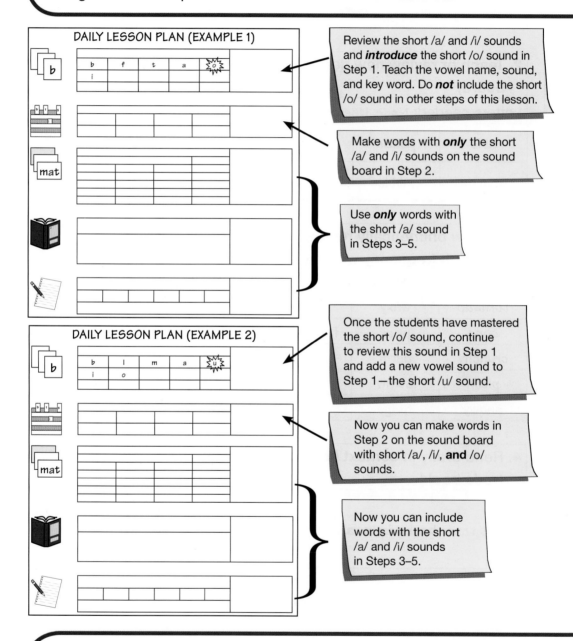

DAILY LESSON PLAN (EXAMPLE 1)

Review the short /a/ and /i/ sounds and *introduce* the short /o/ sound in Step 1. Teach the vowel name, sound, and key word. Do *not* include the short /o/ sound in other steps of this lesson.

Make words with *only* the short /a/ and /i/ sounds on the sound board in Step 2.

Use *only* words with the short /a/ sound in Steps 3–5.

DAILY LESSON PLAN (EXAMPLE 2)

Once the students have mastered the short /o/ sound, continue to review this sound in Step 1 and add a new vowel sound to Step 1—the short /u/ sound.

Now you can make words in Step 2 on the sound board with short /a/, /i/, **and** /o/ sounds.

Now you can include words with the short /a/ and /i/ sounds in Steps 3–5.

> Once students can make words with the short /o/ sound on the sound board (as shown above in Example 2), you are ready to include words with this sound in *all* steps of the lesson. The same procedure is used when introducing each new vowel, final "e" syllable, vowel team, or vowel + *r* pattern.

Appendix B
Trade Books

Here is a list of trade books that has been used with students working in different levels of the program. These books have not been "leveled" using any formal criteria. They have been suggested by teachers using the program. Feel free to add your favorite books to the list.

Red and Orange Level Trade Books

Title	Authors
A Birthday Basket for Tia	Pat Mora
And I Mean It, Stanley	Crosby Bonsall
Barbie: One Pink Shoe	Salile Orr
Bears Are Curious	Joyce Milton
Benny's Big Bubble	Jane O'Connor
The Best Fall of All	Laura Godwin
Bigmama's	Donald Crews
The Big Snowball	Wendy Cheyette Lewison
Bright Eyes, Brown Skin	Cheryl Willis Hudson
The Cat That Sat	Marie Vinje
City Cats, Country Cats	Barbara Shook Hazen
Corduroy	Don Freeman

Digby	Barbara Shook Hazen
Diving Dolphin	Karen Wallace
Dizzy's Bird Watch (Bob the Builder)	Alison Inches
Don't Wake the Baby	Wendy Cheyette Lewison
The Fat Cat Sat on the Mat	Nurit Karlin
First Grade Friends: The Gym Day Winner	Grace Maccarone
Happy Birthday, Danny the Dinosaur	Syd Hoff
Hats, Hats, Hats	Ann Morris
Hop on Pop	Dr. Seuss
Hot Dog	Molly Coxe
How Many Fish?	Caron Lee Cohen
Hush!	Minfong Ho
In a Dark, Dark House	Jennifer Dussling
Jack and Rick	David McPhail
Lots of Hearts	Maryann Cocca-Leffler
More Spaghetti, I Say!	Rita Golden Gelman
Mouse Makes Words	Kathryn Heling
Oh, Cats! (and other My First I Can Read Books)	Nola Buck
On My Way to Buy Eggs	Chih-Yuan Chen
One Fish Two Fish Red Fish Blue Fish	Dr. Seuss
Oscar Otter	Nathaniel Benchley
Picky Nicky	Cathy and Mark Dubowski
Pizza Party	Grace Maccarone
Rick is Sick	Daniel McPhail
Sid and Sam	Nola Buck
Silly Willy	Maryann Cocca-Leffler
Space Kid	Roberta Edwards
Splish Splash	Sarah Weeks

430

Surprise Puppy	Judith Walker-Hodge
Todd's Box	Paula Sullivan
Trouble at the Bridge	Marie Birkinshaw
What Day Is It?	Pattie Trimble
Who Took the Farmer's Hat?	Joan L. Nodset
Wiley Learns to Spell	Betsy Lewin

Yellow and Green Level Trade Books

Title	Authors
Addie Meets Max	Joan Robins
Addie's Bad Day	Joan Robins
All Tutus Should be Pink	Sheri Brownrigg
Amelia Bedelia Helps Out	Peggy Parish
Amelia Bedelia Goes Camping	Peggy Parish
Amelia Bedelia and the Surprise Shower	Peggy Parish
Angus and the Cat	Marjorie Flack
Arthur's Reading Race	Marc Brown
Babe the Sheep Pig: Oops, Pig!	Shana Corey
Bike Lesson, The (The Berenstain Bears)	Stan and Jan Berenstain
Black Snowman, The	Phil Mendez
Bringing the Rain to Kapiti Plain	Verna Aardema
Bunny Slipper Mystery	Jennifer Dussling
Caps for Sale	Esphyr Slobodkina
Case of the Hungry Stranger, The	Crosby Bonsall
Case of the Cat's Meow, The	Crosby Bonsall
Case of the Scaredy Cats, The	Crosby Bonsall
Cat in the Hat, The	Dr. Seuss

Halloween Parade	Harriet Ziefert
Harry and the Lady Next Door	Gene Zion
Henry and Mudge	Cynthia Rylant
Hundred Penny Box, The	Sharon Bell Mathis
I Love Cats	Catherine Matthias
I Spy	Jean Marzollo
Jamaica Tag-Along	Juanita Havill
Kate Skates	Jane O'Connor
Kenny and the Little Kickers	Claudio Marzollo
Kit and Kat	Tomie dePaola
Lad to the Rescue	Margo Lundell
Legend of the Indian Paintbrush, The	Tomie dePaola
Little Bill Best Way to Play	Bill Cosby
Little Bill One Dark and Scary Night	Bill Cosby
Little Bill Treasure Hunt	Bill Cosby
Lon Po Po	Ed Young
Magic Porridge Pot	Harriet Ziefert
Martha Blah Blah	Susan Meddaugh
Martha Calling	Susan Meddaugh
Martha Speaks	Susan Meddaugh
Morris and Boris at the Circus	B. Wiseman
Morris the Mouse	B. Wiseman
Mouse Soup	Arnold Lobel
Mrs. Brice's Mice	Syd Hoff
Nate the Great Goes Down in the Dumps	Marjorie Weinman Sharmat
Nate the Great and the Musical Note	Marjorie Weinman Sharmat
Nate the Great and the Sticky Case	Marjorie Weinman Sharmat
Nate the Great	Marjorie Weinman Sharmat

Triplet Trouble and the Bicycle Race	Dabbie Dadey
Two Silly Trolls	Nancy Jewell
Where Does the Teacher Live?	Paula Kurzband Feder
Whistle for Willie	Ezra Jack Keats
Willie's Wonderful Pet	Mel Cebulash

Blue and Purple Level Trade Books

Title	Authors
Aah! Real Monsters: Hide and Scare	Molly Wigand
Aah! Real Monsters: Monster Camp Out	Molly Wigand
Adirondack Kids	Justin Van Riper and Gary Van Riper
Adirondack Kids: Rescue on Bald Mountain	Justin Van Riper and Gary Van Riper
Adirondack Kids: The Lost Lighthouse	Justin Van Riper and Gary Van Riper
Adventures of Max the Minnow, The	William Boniface
Aladdin and the Magic Lamp	Deborah Hautzig
All Star Fever	Matt Christopher
Amazing Bone	William Steig
Amelia Bedelia, Teach Us	Peggy Parish
Arthur's New Puppy	Marc Brown
Arthur's Tooth	Marc Brown
Arthur's Chicken Pox	Marc Brown
Backstage Pass	Mercer Mayer
Bailey School Kids Joke Book, The	D. Dadey and M.T. Jones
Basket Counts	Matt Christopher

Berenstain Bears in Maniac Mansion	Stan and Jan Berenstain
Box Turtle at Long Pond	William T. George
Brave Irene	William Steig
Brave Sheila Rae, The	Kevin Henkes
Bringing Rain to Kapiti Plain	Verna Aardema
Bug's Life, A: Can You Find the Difference?	Nancy Parent
Cam Jansen and the Ghostly Mystery	David A. Adler
Cam Jansen and the Mystery of the Gold Coins	David A. Adler
Camp Knock Knock	Betsy Duffey
Catch that Pass	Matt Christopher
Choose Your Own Adventure: You Are Invisible	Susan Saunders
Choose Your Own Adventure: Stranded!	Sara Compton
Clue Jr.: The Case of the Secret Message	Parker C. Hinter
Clue Jr.: The Case of the Stolen Jewel	Parker C. Hinter
Commander Toad and the Big Black Hole	Jane Yolen
Commander Toad in Space	Jane Yolen
Critters of the Night: Kiss of the Mermaid	Erica Farber
Critters of the Night: Midnight Snack	Mercer Mayer
Doctor DeSoto	William Steig
Doctor DeSoto Goes to Africa	William Steig
Double Trouble in Walla Walla	Andrew Clements
Drummer Hoff	Barbara Emberley
Five Goofy Ghosts	Judith Bauer Stamper
Flossie and the Fox	Patricia McKissack
Franklin's New Friend	Paulette Bourgeois
Friends of a Feather	Arlen Cohn
Ghost of Goose Island	Mercer Mayer
Giant's Toe	Brock Cole

Graveyard Creeper Mystery #1:	
Swamp of the Hideous Zombies	Geoffrey Hayes
Graveyard Creeper Mystery #2:	
House of the Horrible Ghosts	Geoffrey Hayes
Hardy Boys: Extreme Danger	Franklin W. Dixon
Hardy Boys: Running on Fumes	Franklin W. Dixon
Hardy Boys: Boardwalk Bust	Franklin W. Dixon
Hardy Boys: Trouble in Paradise	Franklin W. Dixon
Haunting of Grade Three, The	Grace Maccarone
Horrible Harry in Room 2B	Suzy Kline
Horrible Harry and the Ant Invasion	Suzy Kline
Horrible Harry and the Kickball Wedding	Suzy Kline
Invisible Inc. #1: The Schoolyard Mystery	Elizabeth Levy
Invisible Inc. #2: The Mystery of the Missing Dog	Elizabeth Levy
Invisible Inc. #3: The Snack Attack Mystery	Elizabeth Levy
Junie B. Jones, First Grade (At Last!)	Barbara Park and Denise Brunkus
Junie B. Jones, First Grader: Toothless Wonder	Barbara Park and Denise Brunkus
Junie B. Jones, First Grader: Boss of Lunch	Barbara Park and Denise Brunkus
Little Polar Bear, Take Me Home	Hans de Beer
Lucky Baseball Bat	Matt Christopher
Mr. Putter and Tabby Pour the Tea	Cynthia Rylant
Mr. Putter and Tabby Pick the Pears	Cynthia Rylant
Mummy's Curse	Mercer Mayer
Mystery in Bugtown	William Boniface
An Otto & Uncle Tooth Adventure:	
The Curse of the Cobweb Queen	Geoffrey Hayes

Title	Author
An Otto & Uncle Tooth Adventure: The Secret of Foghorn Island	Geoffrey Hayes
Pinky and Rex and the Bully	James Howe
Pinky and Rex and the Double-Dad Weekend	James Howe
Pioneer Bear	Joan Sandin
Rugrats: The Bestest Mom	Susan Hood
Rugrats: Junk, Sweet Junk	Molly Wigand
Rugrats: Rugrats Blast Off!	Stephanie Pierre
Scooby-Doo! Map in the Mystery Machine	Gail Herman
Second-Grade Ape	Daniel Pinkwater
Secret Garden, The	Deborah Hautzig
Sharks	M. Oakley
Shrek	William Steig
Soccer Sam	Jean Marzollo
Stan the Hot Dog Man	Ethel and Leonard Kessler
Sylvester and the Magic Pebble	William Steig
Ten Little Dinosaurs	Pattie Schnetzler
There's an Ant in Anthony	Bernard Most
Tight Times	Barbara Shook Hazen
When the Giants Came to Town	Marcia Leonard
White Snow, Bright Snow	Alvin Tresselt

Nonfiction and Poetry

Title	Authors
A. Nonny Mouse Writes Again: Poems Selected by Jack Prelutsky	Jack Prelutsky
Amazing Animal Babies	Christopher Maynard

Appendix C
Frequently
Asked Questions

1. How do I introduce this program to my students?

We recommend that you introduce the Five-Step Plan by having a small group do an abbreviated lesson using just one of the five steps a day for the first week (especially if you are working with first-grade students at the beginning of the year).

For example, on Monday, you might complete just Step 1, reviewing sound–symbol associations. The next day, students could be introduced to the sound board and could practice manipulating the cards to make simple words. By introducing one step each day, the students become familiar with the materials and the procedures used for each step and are better prepared to do a complete lesson.

You should use your judgment about whether this gradual introduction of the steps is necessary for your students.

2. What *do* I *do* with the rest of my class when I am using the program with small groups?

If you are using this program in the general education classroom, you will probably be using it with one or more of your small groups during the English Language Arts (ELA) block.

It is important during the beginning of the year to establish procedures for independent work at centers or work stations around the room. This will help you have quiet time during ELA to meet with small groups for reading instruction.

We have included a few ideas and directions for games in Step 3 of the Red Level. These games can be adapted for use at centers or work stations to review the phonetically regular words (PRWs) and/or high frequency words (HFWs) taught during the lesson.

This program also has been used by teaching assistants, reading teachers, and special education teachers. If you have support staff in your room during ELA time, these staff members can use this program with one of your small groups.

3. There are six levels of this program. Is there one level that is more difficult than any of the others?

This depends on your particular students or group. Students enter the program with different skills. For some students, the first level—the Red Level—is challenging. Learning to read and spell closed syllables (e.g., *cat, hip, shop*) will be new learning for some students and for others it will be review. This means that groups will progress through each level at different rates.

In general, we have found that once students have the foundation skills (i.e., can read and spell closed-, open-, and final "e" syllable patterns) taught in the Red, Orange, and Yellow Levels, they progress more quickly through the remaining levels of the manual.

4. Are there prepared lesson plans for this program?

Complete lesson plans are not provided because we want each teacher to have maximum opportunity for differentiated instruction. Each day on your lesson plan, you will be noting individual needs based on the responses of your students to each step in the lesson. Your notes will give you information that will inform the lessons for the rest of the week. This will help you know what to reteach, review, skip, or extend.

To make it easier for you to individualize your lesson plans for each group, we have provided materials both in the book and on the accompanying CD-ROM ⊙. In the text of each level of the program, you will find lists of sounds, phonetically regular words, and high frequency words. In the Additional Materials section of each level of the program, there are word lists, sample sound board lists, and sample dictation exercises. On the CD-ROM ⊙, word cards are already made—you only need to print them.

Although we have provided lists of both decodable books and trade books, you are free to substitute whatever reading materials are available to you. This makes it possible to use this program with any reading series and, again, provides maximum flexibility to individualize instruction for your groups.

On the CD-ROM ⊙, there are blank lesson plan forms. The lesson plans you write for each group can be used or adapted for other groups that you are currently teaching or will be teaching later in the year.

5. Can I switch the order of the steps? Can I leave out steps?

It is important to note that the steps build on one another. The order of Steps 1–5 is the same order that has been adhered to most of the time in the research studies that provide the foundation for this program.

The lesson begins in Step 1 [b] with students learning and reviewing individual letter sounds. In Step 2 ▦ students use these letter sounds to construct words on the sound board and practice reading these words accurately.

Step 3 `mat` focuses on reading both phonetically regular and high frequency words accurately and fluently, whereas in Step 4 students utilize the skills they have learned in the first three steps to read connected text. Finally, in Step 5 students practice spelling words using the patterns from previous steps in the lesson.

We recognize that lessons may need to be altered due to time constraints. You might find more time for oral reading as the students progress through the program by altering the number of minutes spent on earlier steps.

For example, on a day when you are not adding anything new to the sound board in Step 2 or on a day when you are not adding any new pattern to the word cards in Step 3, you may be able to spend less time on those steps and more time on oral reading.

Another way to find more time for oral reading is to use either the sound board or dictation (but not both) when you are in the last levels (Blue and Purple) of the program and are not introducing as many new skills on the sound board. In the earlier levels—Red, Orange, and Yellow—it is important to use the sound board and do dictation every day.

Teachers in our studies have suggested that there are times when the lesson flows better when they do dictation (Step 5) before oral reading (Step 4). This allows the teacher to extend the oral reading, especially when the students are reading longer texts (e.g., chapter books).

6. In the manual, there is an emphasis on developing fluency. Are there grade-level guidelines that I can use to determine whether my students are reading at an appropriate rate for their grade level?

A number of researchers have published tables that can be used as guidelines when you are monitoring the fluency of your students. The most recent and detailed guidelines that we have found were developed by Hasbrouck and Tindal (2006). Table 1 on the next page was adapted from their article. This table can serve as a guide for grade-level norms based on reading of connected text measured at three different points in the school year.

Table 1. Hasbrouck and Tindal's oral reading fluency norms for Grades 1–4

Percentile	Words correct per minute		
	Fall	Winter	Spring
Grade 1			
90	—	81	111
75	—	47	82
50	—	23	53
25	—	12	28
10	—	6	15
Grade 2			
90	106	125	142
75	79	100	117
50	51	72	89
25	25	42	61
10	11	18	31
Grade 3			
90	128	146	162
75	99	120	137
50	71	92	107
25	44	62	78
10	21	36	48
Grade 4			
90	145	166	180
75	119	139	152
50	94	112	123
25	68	87	98
10	45	61	72

Source: Hasbrouck and Tindal (2006).

7. Every lesson includes dictation. Can this be considered a student's spelling program?

To some extent, the answer to this question will depend on the philosophy of your school. One goal of this program is to help students understand the relationship between reading and spelling. We want students to know that once they have learned to read words with a particular syllable pattern, they can also spell many of the words with that pattern. Spelling is not arbitrary.

For students who have not had success in the traditional classroom spelling program, the words used in daily dictation might constitute a more appropriate spelling program, especially during the early stages of learning to read.

8. Do reading and spelling always improve at the same rate?

Teachers have found that for many students using this program, reading and spelling inform each other at the beginning stages of instruction. That is, students are taught that they can spell the phonetically regular words (PRWs) they can read and that they can read the phonetically regular words they can spell when they are learning closed syllables (e.g., *spin*) and final "e" syllables (e.g., *spine*). These syllable types are taught in the first three levels of the program—Red, Orange, and Yellow.

When students start to learn vowel teams, spelling becomes a more difficult process because there are multiple ways to spell a single sound. For example, students may be able to read the word *rain,* but when they are asked to spell the word, they have to make a choice between using a vowel team (*rain*) or a final "e" (*rane*).

As students gain more experience with reading, they become more familiar with conventional spellings and making the correct choice becomes easier. Students begin to notice that spelling *rain* as *rane* does not look right. On the sound board and in dictation, we provide guided practice to help students think about the sounds and syllable patterns they are using as they spell words.

References and Suggested Resources

Adams, M.J. (1990). *Beginning to read: Thinking and learning about print.* Cambridge, MA: The MIT Press.

Adams, M.J., Foorman, B.R., Lundberg, I., & Beeler, T. (1998). *Phonemic awareness in young children.* Baltimore: Paul H. Brookes Publishing Co.

Ball, E.W., & Blachman, B.A. (1991). Does phoneme awareness training in kindergarten make a difference in early word recognition and developmental spelling? *Reading Research Quarterly, 26*(1), 49–66.

Bear, D.R., Invernizzi, M., Templeton, S., & Johnston, F. (2000). *Words their way: Word study for phonics, vocabulary, and spelling instruction.* Columbus, OH: Merrill.

Beck, I.L., & McKeown, M.G. (2001). Text talk: Capturing the benefits of read-aloud experiences for young children. *The Reading Teacher, 55*(1), 10–20.

Beck, I.L., McKeown, M.G., & Kucan, L. (2003, Spring). Taking delight in words: Using oral language to build young children's vocabularies. In *American Educator.* Retrieved July 14, 2005, from http://www.aft.org/pubs-reports/american_educator/spring2003/words.html

Biemiller, A. (2003, Spring). Oral comprehension sets the ceiling on reading comprehension. In *American Educator.* Retrieved July 14, 2005, from http://www.aft.org/pubs-reports/american_educator/spring2003/biemiller.html

Blachman, B.A. (1987). An alternative classroom reading program for learning disabled and other low-achieving children. In R. Bowler (Ed.), *Intimacy with language: A forgotten basic in teacher education* (pp. 49–55). Baltimore: Orton Dyslexia Society.

Blachman, B.A. (Ed.). (1997). *Foundations of reading acquisition and dyslexia: Implications for early intervention.* Mahwah, NJ: Lawrence Erlbaum Associates.

Blachman, B.A. (2000). Phonological awareness. In M.L. Kamil, P.B. Mosenthal, P.D. Pearson, & R. Barr (Eds.), *Handbook of reading research* (Vol. 3). Mahwah, NJ: Lawrence Erlbaum Associates.

Blachman, B.A., Ball, E., Black, R., & Tangel, D.M. (1994). Kindergarten teachers develop phoneme awareness in low-income, inner-city classrooms: Does it make a difference? *Reading and Writing: An Interdisciplinary Journal, 6,* 1–18.

Blachman, B.A., Ball, E., Black, R., & Tangel, D.M. (2000). *Road to the code: A phonological awareness program for young children.* Baltimore: Paul H. Brookes Publishing Co.

Blachman, B.A., Schatschneider, C., Fletcher, J.M., Francis, D.J., Clonan, S.M., Shaywitz, B.A., et al. (2004). Effects of intensive reading remediation for second and third graders and a 1-year follow-up. *Journal of Educational Psychology, 96*(3), 444–461.

Blachman, B.A., Tangel, D.M., Ball, E.W., Black, R., & McGraw, C.K. (1999). Developing phonological awareness and word recognition skills: A two-year intervention with low-income, inner-city children. *Reading and Writing: An Interdisciplinary Journal, 11,* 239–273.

Block, C.C., & Pressley, M. (Eds.). (2002). *Comprehension instruction: Research-based best practices.* New York: Guilford Press.

Burns, M.S., Griffin, P., & Snow, C.E. (1999). *Starting out right: A guide to promoting children's reading success.* Washington, DC: National Academies Press.

Catts, H., & Kamhi, A. (Eds.). (2005). *Language and reading disabilities.* Boston: Allyn & Bacon.

Chard, D.J., Vaughn, S., & Tyler, B.J. (2002). A synthesis of research on effective interventions for building reading fluency with elementary students with learning disabilities. *Journal of Learning Disabilities, 35*(5), 386–406.

Cunningham, A.E., Stanovich, K.E., & Stanovich, P.J. (2004). Disciplinary knowledge of K–3 teachers and their knowledge calibration in the domain of early literacy. *Annals of Dyslexia, 54*(1), 139–167.

DeBruin-Parecki, A. (2000). *Helping your child become a reader.* Washington, DC: U.S. Department of Education, Office of Educational Research and Improvement.

Dickinson, D.K., & Neuman, S.B. (Eds.). (2006). *Handbook of early literacy* (Vol. 2). New York: Guilford Press.

Dickinson, D.K., & Tabors, P.O. (Eds.). (2001). *Beginning literacy with language:* Young children learning at home and school. Baltimore: Paul H. Brookes Publishing Co.

Ehri, L.C. (2005). Learning to read words: Theory, findings, and issues. *Scientific Studies of Reading, 9*(2), 167–188.

Ehri, L.C., Nunes, S.R., Stahl, S.A., & Willows, D.M. (2001). Systematic phonics instruction helps students learn to read: Evidence from the National Reading Panel's meta-analysis. *Review of Educational Research, 71,* 393–447.

Fletcher, J.M., Foorman, B.R., Boudousquie, A., Barnes, M.A., Schatschneider, C., & Francis, D.J. (2002). Assessment of reading and learning disabilities: A research-based intervention-oriented approach. *Journal of School Psychology, 40,* 27–63.

Fletcher, J.M., Lyon, G.R., Fuchs, L.S., & Barnes, M.A. (2006). *Learning disabilities: From identification to intervention.* New York: Guilford Press.

Foorman, B.R. (Ed.). (2003). *Preventing and remediating reading difficulties: Bringing science to scale.* Timonium, MD: York Press.

Foorman, B.R., & Torgesen, J. (2001). Critical elements of classroom and small-group instruction promote reading success in all children. *Learning Disabilities Research & Practice, 16*(4), 203–212.

Fry, E., & Kress, D. (2006). *The reading teacher's book of lists* (5th ed.). New York: John Wiley & Sons.

Fuchs, D., & Fuchs, L.S. (2006). Introduction to response to intervention: What, why, and how valid is it? *Reading Research Quarterly, 41*(1), 93–99.

Hall, S.L., & Moats, L.C. (1999). *Straight talk about reading: How parents can make a difference in the early years.* Chicago: Contemporary Books.

Hasbrouck, J. (2006, Summer). Drop everything and read—but how? *American Educator,* 22–29, 30–31, 46–47.

Hasbrouck, J., & Tindal, G.A. (2006). Oral reading fluency norms: A valuable assessment tool for reading teachers. *The Reading Teacher, 59,* 636–644.

Hiebert, E.H., & Kamil, M.L. (Eds.). (2005). *Teaching and learning vocabulary: Bringing reading to practice.* Mahwah, NJ: Lawrence Erlbaum Associates.

Hirsch, E.D. (2003, Spring). Reading comprehension requires knowledge—of words and the world. *American Educator,* 10–29.

Johnston, F.R., Invernizzi, M., & Juel, C. (1998). *Book Buddies: Guidelines for volunteer tutors of emergent and early readers.* New York: Guilford Press.

Juel, C. (1994). *Learning to read and write in one elementary school.* New York: Springer-Verlag.

Kamil, M.L., Mosenthal, P.B., Pearson, P.D., & Barr, R. (2000). *Handbook of reading research: Vol. 3.* Mahwah, NJ: Lawrence Erlbaum Associates.

Kuhn, M.R., & Stahl, S.A. (2003). Fluency: A review of developmental and remedial practices. *Journal of Educational Psychology, 95*(2), 3–21.

Liberman, I.Y., & Shankweiler, D. (1991). Phonology and beginning reading: A tutorial. In L. Rieben & C.A. Perfetti (Eds.), *Learning to read: Basic research and its implications* (pp. 3–17). Mahwah, NJ: Lawrence Erlbaum Associates.

Lyon, G.R. (2002). Reading development, reading difficulties, and reading instruction: Educational and public health issues. *Journal of School Psychology, 1,* 3–6.

McCardle, P., & Chhabra, V. (Eds.). (2004). *The voice of evidence in reading research.* Baltimore: Paul H. Brookes Publishing Co.

Moats, L.C. (1995). The missing foundation in teacher preparation. *American Educator, 19*(9), 43–51.

Moats, L.C. (2000). *Speech to print: Language essentials for teachers.* Baltimore: Paul H. Brookes Publishing Co.

National Institute of Child Health and Human Development. (2000). *Report of the National Reading Panel. Teaching children to read: An evidence-based assessment of the scientific research literature on reading and its implications for reading instruction: Reports of the subgroups* (NIH Publication No. 00-4754). Washington, DC: U.S. Government Printing Office. Also available on-line: http://www.nichd.nih.gov/publications/nrp/report.htm

Pikulski, J., & Chard, D.J. (2005). Fluency: Bridge between decoding and reading comprehension. *The Reading Teacher, 58*(6), 510–519.

Rayner, K., Foorman, B.R., Perfetti, C.A., Pesetsky, D., & Seidenberg, M.S. (2001). How psychological science informs the teaching of reading. *Psychological Science, 2*(2), 31–74.

Shavelson, R.J., & Towne, L. (Eds.). (2003). *Scientific research in education.* Washington, DC: National Academies Press.

Snow, C.E., Burns, M.S., & Griffin, P. (Eds.). (1998). *Preventing reading difficulties in young children.* Washington, DC: National Academies Press.

Snowling, M.J., & Hulme, C. (Eds.). (2005). *The science of reading: A handbook.* Oxford, United Kingdom: Blackwell.

Stahl, K.A. (2004). Proof, practice, and promise: Comprehension strategy instruction in the primary grades. *The Reading Teacher, 57*(7), 598–609.

Stanovich, K.E. (1986). Matthew effects in reading: Some consequences of individual differences in the acquisition of literacy. *Reading Research Quarterly, 21,* 360–407.

Stanovich, K.E. (2000). *Progress in understanding reading: Scientific foundations and new frontiers.* New York: Guilford Press.

Tangel, D.M., & Blachman, B.A. (1992). Effect of phoneme awareness instruction on kindergarten children's invented spelling. *Journal of Reading Behavior, 24,* 233–261.

Tangel, D.M., & Blachman, B.A. (1995). Effect of phoneme awareness instruction on kindergarten children's invented spelling of first grade children: A one year follow-up. *Journal of Reading Behavior, 27,* 153–185.

Torgesen, J.K. (2004, Fall). Avoiding the devastating downward spiral: The evidence that early intervention prevents reading failure. *American Educator,* 6–47.

Treiman, R. (1993). *Beginning to spell.* New York: Oxford University Press.

Vellutino, F.R., Scanlon, D.M., Sipay, E.R., Small, S.G., Pratt, A., Chen, R.S., et al. (1996). Cognitive profiles of difficult to remediate and readily remediated poor readers: Early intervention as a vehicle for distinguishing between cognitive and experiential deficits as basic causes of specific reading disability. *Journal of Educational Psychology, 88*(4), 607–638.

Wasik, B.A., Bond, M.A., & Hindman, A. (2006). The effects of a language and literacy intervention on Head Start children and teachers. *Journal of Educational Psychology, 98*(1), 63–74.

Web Sites to Explore

http://www.nifl.gov/partnershipforreading
The Partnership for Reading is a collaborative effort of the National Institute for Literacy, the National Institute of Child Health and Human Development, the U.S. Department of Education, and the U.S. Department of Health and Human Services. This web site provides information on research about reading instruction, materials (for teachers and parents) that you can download, links to other resources, and answers to questions about reading instruction.

http://www.fcrr.org
The Florida Center for Reading Research provides a wealth of evidence-based materials. In addition to offering materials that teachers can download, the site includes answers to questions about research-based instruction and assessment, data from successful schools, and PowerPoint presentations by Dr. Joseph Torgesen, that can be used for professional development.